Dedication

This book is dedicated to all the men and women I've met over the years who are doing personal work to heal their emotional wounds, recover their true selves, and grow as men and women so they can more fully embody the mature masculine and feminine.

Warrior, Magician, Lover, King

A Guide To The Male Archetypes Updated For The 21st Century

Rod Boothroyd

Warrior, Magician, Lover, King: A Guide To The Male Archetypes Updated For The 21st Century

First Edition Published 2018 by Sovereign Books Ltd

No part of this book may be reproduced by any mechanical, photographic or electronic process, nor in the form of a photographic recording. It may not be copied or transmitted electronically or otherwise either for private or public use, other than for the purposes of "fair use" as brief quotations or critical analysis incorporated in articles and reviews, without prior written permission of the publisher.

The moral rights of the author have been asserted in accordance with the Copyright, Designs and Patents Act, 1988.

Copyright © 2018 Rod Boothroyd & Sovereign Books Ltd

sales@sovereignbookpublishing.com

All rights reserved. No reproduction without permission except for the use of short extracts in illustration or analysis.

ISBN-13: 978-1722820893
ISBN-10: 1722820896

Contents

	Acknowledgements	1
1	The Archetypes Within Us	3
2	The Warrior Archetype	15
3	The Magician Archetype	55
4	The Lover Archetype	83
5	The Sovereign Archetype	113
6	Your Shadow Uncovered: Exploring Your Unknown Inner World	155
7	Emotional Process Work: Becoming Who You Were Always Meant To Be	173
8	Resources: Places To Work On Your Shadow	179

Acknowledgements

I'm deeply indebted to the late Robert Moore and Douglas Gillette for their pioneering work on the male archetypes. Their books provided men with a guide to the male psyche which has done much to illuminate the way men think and feel in society today. Beyond them, of course, lies the profound influence of Carl Jung, father of archetypal theory. More recently, Robert Bly and other significant contributors to the modern men's movement have massively advanced our understanding of maleness and masculinity.

I am also grateful to Cliff Barry, who has combined a number of different ideas and developed the practice of Shadow Work. He has produced what I believe to be one of the most effective approaches for human growth and development currently available to us.

My curiosity and passion to learn and understand more about the human psyche is fostered by support from the men who join me each week in our various men's groups. And my gratitude also goes to my clients, both in group work and one to one work, who have taught me the true meaning of humanity and compassion.

In the production of this book, I have been guided and helped, directly and indirectly, by my discussions and work with my colleagues Diarmaid Fitzpatrick, Ed Rooke, and Marianne Hill. My thanks also go to Richard Grey and Marianne Hill for their assistance with proof reading.

And finally, I thank my original teachers and therapists, Bob Cooke and Richard Erskine, for the gifts which they have so generously given me, in so many different forms.

Chapter 1

The Archetypes Within Us

We look like separate individuals, each of us walking around in our own body. Despite this appearance of separation we have more in common than we realize, including some primal "blueprints" or "archetypes" laid down deep in our unconscious minds. These archetypes are templates or patterns which shape the way we think, feel and behave. And because they're derived from shared concepts, images and representations of the world and the people in it, they're something we all instinctively recognize as a fundamental part of our humanity.

Take an example: if I say the word Warrior, you instantly know what I mean. And the same is true if I speak of a Magician or a King or a Father or Mother. These are all human archetypes, each of which can take many different forms.

Being human, we share the same genetic inheritance. And so we also share the same feelings, emotions, and ways of thinking. Sure, we differ in physical appearance, but essentially our genetic inheritance is one and the same – it's human. No wonder we all instinctively understand the idea of human archetypes. Whether these archetypes are male and female, young or old, we intuitively know what they are, how they operate, and what role they play in our lives.

Carl Jung was probably the first Western psychologist to recognize that archetypes are something we all have in common; he believed the energy of archetypes resided in what he called the "collective unconscious". Nowadays most people see archetypes as being stored in the unconscious mind rather like permanent programs etched into the memory of a computer chip. The unconscious seems to have unlimited storage capacity, holding not just our archetypal programming but perhaps also a memory of every event that's ever happened to us. It also holds all the basic biological "programs" we need to stay alive including those which control digestion, respiration, circulation of the blood, and the chemical balance in our tissues, among many others.

So what do archetypes actually do for us? Perhaps it's most useful to think of them as genetically determined potentials or possibilities for different aspects of our personality. The exact way in which a particular archetype will be expressed in each of us will be influenced by our individual experience of life and the culture in which we live.

Over the years, different psychologists have come up with different names for human archetypes. Some of them we would all recognize: to take another example, we all intuitively know what is meant when we hear of the female archetype of the Mother. If you pause for a moment to consider what the word "Mother" means to you, you'll most likely have conjured up your version of the Mother archetype in your mind.

Equally, you probably also have a sense of what the Wise Elder archetype might mean in a man or a woman. And you will certainly know how a King or Queen archetype might look.

The important point about these archetypes is that they're common to all humanity. They're like an internal foundation upon which every man and every woman builds their own particular experience of life. To make the point again, the way in which each archetype finds its expression in an individual man or woman will be shaped by what they learn for themselves, what they learned about life from their parents, and influences from their cultural background.

Although there are many different archetypes which describe aspects of human experience, there are four fundamental archetypes which embody the most important parts of our personalities with extraordinary precision.

These four archetypes are the Sovereign (the King or Queen), the Warrior, the Magician, and the Lover. Many writers have adapted those names and come up with words they believe are more representative of the energy in each archetype. For example:

Sovereign = Leader, Chieftain, Chairman, Director, Elder
Warrior   = Action Taker, Worker
Magician = Thinker, Wise Man or Wise Woman, Sage
Lover   = Sensor, Feeler, Connector

However for me the original names really sum up the main areas of our personality. They exist within each one of us almost like different individuals. Certainly they are separate and distinct areas of your personality and each of them carries a particular energy.

And this is where the concept of archetypes becomes very useful in working with the behaviours that you want to change. In my work with men and women, the most common questions I'm asked, one way or another, are "Why am I behaving this way?" "Why do I feel like this?" and "What can I do to change the way I think, feel, and behave?"

The answer is – start by looking at how you express each of these archetypes. When you do this it becomes easy to see why you're behaving in a certain way and, more importantly, it's much easier to change unhelpful or unwanted behaviours into something that really supports you in your life and in the world.

Here's a brief introduction to each of them. Later we'll look at them in more detail.

The Sovereign Or King

The Sovereign archetype within you is a King. This is the part of you responsible for leadership in your life, creating a vision for your life, and knowing your purpose.

Your Sovereign has responsibility for finding your vision, giving you a sense of purpose and direction in the world, and running your life in the best possible way. This is the part of you that makes (or at least *should* make) the important decisions about how to live your life, what career to follow, where to live, and how to manage your Kingdom, your particular realm.

Your Kingdom might be your family, your business, your circle of friends, your own life, and more. Your Sovereign is the rightful leader in all of them. When his energy is expressed fully your Sovereign makes you a mature, decisive, powerful and potent leader. This means you can – and do – run your life effectively. From that standpoint you can love and bless others, accept them just as they are, and offer compassionate wisdom and guidance to help them achieve their own maturity and fullness of expression.

Every Sovereign throughout history has been responsible for "holding" the wounds of his kingdom and ensuring the safety and protection of the citizens of the realm. In the same way, your own internal Sovereign is responsible for holding your emotional wounds and finding ways for you to grow into your full potential. (We all have emotional wounds which limit us in one way or another. These wounds are a result of the negative life experiences that inevitably happen to each of us from the moment we are born. They prevent us experiencing all our feelings freely, in a natural way. They inhibit the expression of our full potential. In short, they make us less than we really are, less than we have the potential to be.)

The Sovereign is the archetype which produces powerful and respected leaders. Yet where are the powerful and respected leaders in the world today? I see very few true leaders worthy of our respect, while we seem to have plenty of immature leaders who haven't grown into the full expression of their Sovereign archetype.

In fact I believe the most deficient archetype in our world today, and certainly the least expressed, is the Sovereign. Quite why there is such a deficiency of sovereign energy isn't completely clear, but it's certainly a problem for humanity. It's also beginning to look like a problem for the planet on which we live. We'll look in much more detail at sovereign qualities later in the book, along with all the other archetypes.

The Warrior

The Warrior is an archetype which is all about taking action in the world and setting boundaries.

Some people object to the word Warrior because it has such negative connotations in modern society. And Warriors have indeed been creating chaos all around the world for as long as the human race has been in existence.

Yet the Warrior can also be a noble archetype when it's called upon to protect something of value: think of the Samurai Warriors, for example. Samurai fought for just and noble causes, and if their Lord became corrupt or immoral they would seek another master.

However, to operate at his highest level a Warrior needs a strong Sovereign to control him and send him out on missions which serve a purpose. This might be a mission to protect people in the kingdom, to defend the boundaries of the kingdom, or simply to get things done.

Warriors can fight from an offensive or defensive position

depending on what's needed of them. But the world we now live in could well do without the warlike quality of the Warrior. This is why I prefer simply to think of the Warrior in terms of male energy, an energy which is all about taking action in the world, about getting things done. Some people call this archetypal energy "The Worker". Whatever you call it, warrior energy is all about setting boundaries, accomplishing tasks, and achieving objectives.

The Magician

The Magician within you is your internal problem solver, your creative power. He is the one who finds answers to problems and works out how the needs of the Kingdom may be fulfilled. He is the one who kept you safe when you were a child, and he may continue to work as your safeguarder and protector even when you are an adult.

Many names have been used for the Magician archetype including the Sage, the Witch, the Wizard, and a whole lot of other things – Trickster, Wise Woman, Mystic, and so on. They all come down to the same thing: the Magician's main motivation is problem solving and coming up with solutions. This is an archetype concerned with thinking in all its forms – rational thinking, logical thinking, and creative thinking.

This is the archetype which serves the Sovereign as an adviser or counsellor. The Magician finds solutions to problems and creates ways around difficulties; he likes an intellectual challenge. It's an archetype that's abundantly present in the world today, particularly in the world of hi-tech industry and technological development.

As we shall see there are both advantages and disadvantages to the abundance of Magician energy in the world today: in some ways it helps us but in other ways it can be quite destructive. This is because Magicians aren't so much concerned with the emotional consequences of their actions as simply meeting the challenges presented to them.

The Magician is also the part of us which comes up with strategies to keep us safe when we're children. For kids who are raised in less than perfect environments or in downright abusive environments, the part of the Magician we call the Safety Officer or Risk Manager is vital: he creates strategies which keep the child as safe as possible even in circumstances that can't really be controlled. One of the challenges we all face in life, though, is that the Risk Manager continues to play out those strategies for the rest of our lives, even when the need for them has long since passed. This can be unhelpful and limiting, as we'll see when we look at the Magician in more detail later in the book.

The Lover

The Lover is all about the glorious experience of deep emotional connection to another human being. He cares not one whit for boundaries; for him, life is all about unity, connection, flow, and of course finding ways to express those qualities. He values sensuous experience over anything else.

You may think of sex and romantic love when we refer to the Lover archetype but that isn't really what the Lover is all about. The archetypal energy of the Lover is much more primal than the expression of sexuality: it's about establishing connection with other human beings. We are social animals, and when we don't have the opportunity to meet others and connect with them on a social level we may descend into mental disorder and even madness. You see this in prisoners who are kept in solitary confinement.

The Lover is a primal archetype, probably the first one to appear after birth. Our first and most urgent need as a helpless baby is to bond with mother. Our very survival depends on it. Our Lover archetype helps us to do this: it's programmed to connect with other people from the moment we appear in the world. In fact, the power of this drive is immense, yet it's not consciously felt by most people even though it controls much of what we do and how we are in the world as adults.

One of the unavoidable problems with such a powerful urge to bond is that it can never be fully satisfied – in fact it's impossible for any child to have all of his or her needs met perfectly. That would require a perfect parent, and as far as I'm aware there's no such thing. So every one of us is inevitably hurt or wounded to some extent in our Lover archetype.

Unfortunately many children are born into an environment where their needs are barely acknowledged, let alone adequately met. Their lives are subsequently blighted by the pain of connections never made, or made and broken. We'll see how this can affect a person's entire life later in the book. Addictions, dependency and neediness are some of the most common outcomes of emotional wounds in this archetype.

The Nature Of Emotional Wounds

Obviously we do not all have equal amounts of sovereign, magician, lover and warrior energy. This is because what happens to each of us during childhood influences the growth of the archetypes within us in a very individual way.

In an ideal world all these archetypal energies would find a fully mature and balanced expression in each of us so we could all achieve our full potential. In reality we are all emotionally hurt or "wounded" in various ways during childhood, and this wounding can inhibit or transform the way an archetypal energy is expressed later in life.

The good news is that our emotional wounds can be a catalyst for change. They can lead us to seek guidance from counsellors, therapists, and other Magicians who work in the healing arts. Working with your emotional wounds (if you prefer, "healing" them) means you can more fully express your innate potential and become more of the person you were always meant to be. In fact, working with your archetypes can be a fast and effective way to discover how to express every aspect of yourself in a healthy, confident, powerful and uninhibited way.

An experienced facilitator who understands how to access the unbalanced, repressed or shut down energy in your archetypes can help you to restore full potency and balance to each of them. This is an extremely powerful approach to emotional healing and personal growth and development which can transform every area of your life. You can check out how to access this transformational work in the resources section of this book, which you can find on page 179.

Healing your emotional wounds, great or small, is much easier when you have some insight into your archetypes and you know about the idea of "shadow". And that's where we're going right now...

The Shadow

Where there are archetypes there is also shadow. Your shadow is the part of your unconscious where you put all of the energies, emotions, thoughts, feelings and behaviours that for one reason or another were not acceptable when you were a child. Not acceptable, that is, either to you or to the people around you.

Robert Bly described how a child is born into the world with a 360 degree personality – an all-round, complete, whole personality. As Alice Miller put it, this is the child's gift to the world: he arrives in the world "trailing clouds of glory". Fortunate indeed is the child who discovers a world which welcomes his wholeness and glory, the gift of himself just as he is.

Many, perhaps most, children do not. Instead they soon discover their parents do not want the gift they have to offer, at least not in the form on offer. Their parents wanted something different. A boy rather than a girl, or a girl rather than a boy. A quiet baby or a compliant child. A "good" boy or a "feisty" girl. An amenable child, not a defiant, angry one. A placid child, not a needy, demanding one.

And so a child soon learns which parts of himself need to be suppressed for maximum love to be bestowed upon him; and the parts which are not wanted by the world or the people in it usually get shoved forcibly into the child's unconscious, into what Robert Bly aptly termed the "Shadow Bag".

This attempt to suppress those parts of his energy which are not acceptable to the all-powerful adults, siblings, or peers in his world can massively impact every aspect of a child's later life. So much so that one day he (or she) may well arrive at the door of a counsellor or psychotherapist's consulting room. He may be looking for help as he tries to find the parts of himself that he senses are missing, or he may be wondering why he constantly experiences unhelpful and repetitive patterns in his life.

Talking therapies can, without doubt, be a great introduction to self-development work. Yet there is often a point where deeper work is called for, and this may be where the pursuit of one's true self could be made easier by consulting a man or woman trained in what we can call Emotional Process Work or Shadow Work.

Such a "Magician" understands how and why things are put into shadow in the first place, and knows how to get them out again. With this training, the coach, counsellor or therapist will be better able to get the repressed material out of shadow and integrated back where it belongs, in its owner's consciousness. The resources section of this book offers suggestions about where you can find men and women who are experienced in this kind of "archetypal" counselling, coaching and therapy, and who are adept in working with shadow energies.

Later in the book we'll take apart the shadow and look at it from the inside out. For the moment it's convenient to simply think of it as made up of the parts of yourself you attempted to hide, repress and deny as a child. And although the word shadow conjures up darkness, let's not forget that many positive energies are repressed as well.

To take a simple example, children often repress their power, their magnificence, and their glory. These are all qualities that make them stand out and shine in the world – or at least, qualities that *could* make them stand out and shine in the world if they were supported emotionally in their growth through life.

The problem is that our culture can be very hostile to Sovereign energy, particularly in children. The unthinking small-mindedness of parents, other adults, siblings, teachers and friends doesn't necessarily encourage children to show themselves in all their glory. So into the shadow bag goes a child's "golden" qualities as well as his "darker" energies (all of which are a natural part of being human, remember).

There's a big problem here. What you put into shadow doesn't lose its energy – far from it. Imagine a child who puts his anger into shadow because his parents don't like that particular energy in their little boy. Think of a child who suppresses his tears and pain because Dad doesn't like his little boy crying; in fact Dad thinks it shows the boy is a sissy, and somehow the boy knows that, even though Dad doesn't explicitly say it. The message always gets through somehow.

And so to please his all-powerful parents, on whom the child knows his survival depends, the child may well repress his anger, sadness and weakness – or any other quality his parents don't accept or approve of.

But putting these feelings and behaviours out of sight and out of mind into the unconscious mind, into the shadow bag, doesn't take their energy away: in fact their energy can intensify. They are a part of who the child is and they continue to be energetically supported by his psyche.

Over time this energy may grow to a level where it can't be contained any longer by unconscious repression. Then it may emerge unexpectedly and uncontrollably in a distorted form. This is almost always unhelpful or even downright destructive to the child or the adult man whom the child has become.

These shadow energies can make us behave in ways that cause difficulties in our relationships. Shadow energies make us do things which cause embarrassment and shame. They often lead to low self-esteem and self-criticism. They may manifest as strong emotions: anxiety, guilt, depression, shame, rage, jealousy, sadness, and so on. They are irrational. They make us say things we regret and which destroy harmony and goodness in our relationships. We do not understand what comes out of our shadow, and no matter how much we try to control it, nothing ever seems to change.

The point about shadow energies is that they're out of our awareness (it's dark in that shadow bag!) and when they emerge into the light they often do so unexpectedly and unhelpfully. They get in the way of us expressing who we are, getting what we want, telling others what we expect and desire, and expressing our needs. To put it another way, shadow energies stop us being who we truly are.

Our shadow can prevent us from getting into relationships or ruin existing relationships. It can keep us lost in a cycle of addiction, unable to stop self-defeating behaviours. Shadow makes people compulsively behave in ways which are harmful to them and seek out things which are destructive to them, and it all happens in a way they can't understand and which makes no rational sense.

In fact your shadow lies behind every dysfunctional, unhelpful, unexpected and unwanted thought, feeling and behaviour you've ever brought into the world.

And while many of those things don't matter, some of them do, because they get in the way of you living the life you want to be living. So the question naturally arises, "What can I do about all this?"

The answer is to take the energy out of your unconscious and make it conscious; to open up to whatever you've hidden away, out of sight if not out of mind. Then you can transform it into something more useful and helpful that serves you better in your life today.

It's an approach that takes the parts of yourself you stuffed away as a child out of your shadow and brings them back into the light.

And it honours them, heals or transforms them if necessary, makes them into a positive and helpful part of you, and finally integrates them into the essence of who you are today.

There are many names for this approach, including "Healing The Shadow", "Emotional Process Work", and "Shadow Work". Whatever you call it, this is all about getting your sabotaging, holding-back, limiting and now generally unhelpful parts out of shadow and giving you control over them so you can access their energy in a helpful form. In short, these techniques can make your shadow energy available to you in a healthy, emotionally mature way to use in your life today. And if that sounds exciting, so it should!

You'll discover how to step into your power. You'll become more emotionally mature, stronger, more independent, more balanced, and better able to give and receive love.

You'll be better able to set healthy boundaries and you'll become a stronger and more powerful leader in your life. You'll develop the strength and will to get things done more effectively, think more clearly, and stop making harsh judgements about yourself and others.

You'll develop a much easier relationship with love so you can give and receive genuine love freely. In fact just about every other problem that you have in your interactions with other human beings will become more and more manageable and simply melt away over time.

Perhaps you think that sounds too good to be true. But just for a moment imagine how your life might look right now if you'd enjoyed an ideal childhood in which your needs were fully met. A childhood throughout which you were loved and supported unconditionally and where you were allowed to express your personality exactly as you wished. A childhood in which you could grow to embrace all your qualities and values and learn how to manage all the emotional energies within your personality.

Imagine what your life would now be like if you'd had the opportunity to fully access every part of your psyche rather than having to use your energy in repressing parts of yourself that were unwanted or unsafe to express for some reason in your childhood. Do you think that might have made a difference to your life? Yes?

You are absolutely right; your life would most likely have been very different. Now you can bring those changes to life anyway. Through Emotional Process Work, Healing the Shadow, Shadow

Work – call it what you may – you can fully grow into your true self, overcome the blocks of emotional development which have held you back until now, and heal your emotional wounds. And you can do this no matter what stage of life you have reached.

What's even better is that this approach is equally effective for all of us, regardless of gender, sexual orientation, ethnic origin or any other characteristic which appears to separate us. For when we say that in our workshops and one-to-one consultations, "All of you is welcome here", we really mean it. And we mean it because our work focuses on the one thing we all have in common – our humanity. More of that later. For now, let us turn our attention to the archetypes.

Chapter 2

The Warrior Archetype

The Warrior archetype is at the core of every man's being. For many thousands of years our survival as a species has depended on the Warrior archetype. The Warrior archetype gave us the energy to hunt, build homes, battle against hostile tribes, and find ways of surviving in a dangerous world. And because of its power over life and death the Warrior archetype is deep within our genes to this day – it is an essential and unavoidable part of the human male.

When we repress the warrior energy within us we also repress a vital part of our masculinity, and then we can never embody the fullest expression of who we really are. Maybe we even sacrifice some aspects of our soul. Yet at the same time the idea of warrior energy has received a bad rap. Women in particular seem to be uncomfortable with this aspect of the male psyche – and who can blame them?

Look around the world today or consider any time in our history and you will see ample evidence of warfare, slaughter and mutual destruction in ever more sophisticated and monstrous forms.

No wonder this uncontrolled aggression, this uncontrolled warrior energy, has been demonized. Yet demonizing our warrior energy and trying to suppress it, even eliminate it from our society, doesn't seem to have worked too well. Nowadays there seems to be more aggression and more destruction than ever before in the history of humanity, perhaps even extending to the destruction of the planet on which we live.

The problem is that when archetypal warrior energy is repressed rather than embraced, this energy becomes a potent force in our shadow and then it will inevitably erupt from time to time in emotional and physical violence. Alternatively it may be turned inwards and eventually reappear in acts of self-abuse, self-harm or depression.

But such destruction originating in the Warrior archetype is a corrupted and uncontrolled form of this energy. It is not the mature expression of the Warrior which is so necessary for our well-being and survival.

Throughout human history almost every society has had initiation rituals for teenage boys on the brink of manhood. These rituals have put those boys through challenging rites of passage which take them over the threshold of adolescence and step them clearly and undeniably on the road to becoming mature men, men who have total control over their Warrior.

The purpose of these rites of passage has always been very clear: they demonstrate to the arrogant, testosterone-fuelled teenage boy that he is smaller and less powerful than the world around him. He is not, in fact, master of all he surveys. He is not the powerful, all-conquering, all-knowing being he thinks he is.

These rites of passage were, in part, a lesson designed to teach boys how to control their warrior energy and live with respect for their environment and the men and women within that environment.

If you look at the world today I believe you can clearly see that something needs to be transformed within this part of the male psyche. In many ways the male warrior energy we see in the world is destructive, even devastating. But if the Warrior is a universal archetype present within our genetic code then we need to find a way of living with it, not demonizing it. A way of transforming it, not repressing it. We cannot ignore warrior energy simply because it is not to our refined, modern day tastes and sensibilities.

To do this we need to first find how it can serve us and then to discover how to embrace the positive qualities of our Warrior so it can constructively help us in our life and work. This will help to save the human race from the destructive qualities of the Hero archetype (the immature form of the Warrior) and the shadows of the Warrior archetype.

The Warrior In His Fullness

With that in mind, let's look at the powerful qualities of the mature Warrior in his fullness.

Powerful Male Energy

Think of a Warrior's qualities and you might think of aggression. But like the word "Warrior" the word "aggression" has a bad rap. It's a word which evokes thoughts of conflict and violence, of invading someone else's territory. Aggression implies a lack of respect for boundaries and is often seen, perhaps rightly, as a force disruptive to harmony rather than a constructive route to peaceful co-existence.

Those men who have experienced the "red mist" or "bloodlust" will understand how men in combat situations or dangerous situations can be overtaken by a force which seems to go beyond themselves. This is a rage for killing which may be a potential energy within all men.

The ancient civilizations knew this, which is why they had initiation rituals and rites of passage for young men. Nowadays we fear it, with good reason. We may pretend it is not within us, yet in doing so we cut ourselves off from a fundamental part of who we truly are as men.

If we take a step back from this point of view and look at aggression in a different way, we can see it has many valuable and positive qualities. And when we see that, we can start to transform our view of the Warrior archetype by renaming this energy.

So let us think of the energy of the Warrior as simply masculine energy – the kind of energy that gets things done in the world. Then masculine energy, the energy of taking action in the world, becomes the purest and most basic form of the energy we call assertiveness, anger or aggression.

When you see the energy of the Warrior in this light it simply becomes an energizing force that gets us out into the world and motivates us to live fully. It moves us from a position of passivity and defensiveness to one of action and achievement. To put it bluntly, it gets us out of bed in the morning.

And then this energy clearly becomes one of our greatest allies. Truth is, the energetic force of the Warrior archetype with its power to move out into the world and change things, to get things done, is a significant element in your ability to get what you want in life.

Yet if warrior energy is the energy of going out into the world and getting things done, then the question arises: how do you know what level of warrior energy is appropriate in any particular set of circumstances?

For even when your Sovereign has given orders to your Warrior to go out and get things done (as he should be doing), there is still a judgement to be made about the degree of force that is appropriate. This is where the Warrior's quality of discernment comes into play.

Discernment

A Warrior knows what he wants and he knows how to get it done. As he acts he draws authority for his actions from the instructions of his Sovereign. He heeds the wisdom of the Magician archetype for advice on how to achieve his objectives. Yet in his own right your Warrior can also be a master tactician and a cunning strategist.

So the Warrior is no dumb servant of the Sovereign. Ideally he serves your Sovereign because he believes in the rightness and justice of the King's cause.

This is a Warrior tradition: loyalty to a just cause. Samurai Warriors, often held up as a model of Warrior energy, would only serve their Lord for as long as they believed his cause was just and right. When their Lord became corrupt or pursued ignoble aims, true Samurai Warriors would transfer their loyalty to a new Lord – one they could honourably serve in the pursuit of another noble cause.

So a Warrior's discernment is partly about judging whether the cause for which he is fighting is just and right and proper; he might consider whether it benefits the Kingdom and the subjects of the realm. He also needs to bring discernment about the way in which his fight should be taken into the world. To use a military analogy, an army commander might find that a frontal assault is going to cost too many lives or take too much time and too many resources; and so he might decide to adopt guerrilla tactics or guerrilla warfare.

Whatever strategy the Warrior adopts he will certainly know the right moment at which to leap into battle. This discernment tends to be absent in the adolescent boy and young man. Their Warrior energy is invested in the archetype of the Hero.

We'll look at this in more detail in a moment, but essentially the Hero archetype is an undeveloped form of the Warrior archetype in which a boy – or indeed a man still in its grip – does not know his limitations and somehow still believes he has the power to change (or even save) the world single-handed.

By contrast, a mature Warrior has clarity and discernment which he brings to the challenges he's facing. For him, being a Warrior isn't just a physical fight; it's an emotional and mental campaign as well. A mature Warrior needs a mind which is as sharp as his sword, for he must think clearly under pressure. He must assess each situation and take action in the way which is most likely to lead to victory.

If your Warrior is physically weak, his ability to attack and defend as necessary can be developed with the discipline of martial arts and sports such as fencing. These can also be helpful in improving the sharpness and discernment of his thinking. In sports like these, deciding whether to attack or defend from one moment to the next requires split-second decisions applied with unwavering force and total certainty. Such discipline hones both mind and body.

Setting and Protecting Boundaries

One of your Warrior's primary functions is to set boundaries and then protect and defend them. These may be the boundaries of your property, the physical area of land you inhabit, into which you don't permit others to enter without your permission.

However your boundaries can also be intangible. For example, if you set a boundary around your working hours you might refuse a request to work more hours than your contract specifies.

Or you might set a boundary around the way you allow other people to talk to you. You might set a boundary around what is acceptable behaviour on the part of your friends, family, spouse and children. You might set a boundary with your wife or colleague during an argument by telling her that what she's saying, or the way she's saying it, are not acceptable to you. Your Warrior's duty is to make it clear when people in your Kingdom overstep the boundaries of what you're willing to accept.

You may also set boundaries around your emotional space. As a man you may feel the need to retreat into some kind of private personal space. This is often described as going into the "man cave". By withdrawing into a personal space in this way and by setting a boundary about who can come into that space and join you, you're employing your Warrior energy.

You might choose to set a boundary around who you want in your life or what level of involvement you want others to have in particular aspects of your life. You might set a boundary around old relationships or situations whose time has come to an end, so as to exclude them from your future life.

The more you think about this, the more obvious it becomes how essential clear boundaries are to every single one of us and how our internal Warrior is charged with defending and maintaining them.

You probably already know how effectively you keep your own boundaries intact when other people invade them. Perhaps in some areas of your life you maintain better boundaries than in others. It can be difficult, for example, to maintain boundaries with a boss who has power over you.

One thing is certain: a man who doesn't protect his boundaries or who doesn't even know where they lie is likely to be a man who will carry within him a sense of weakness, inadequacy and failure, maybe even cowardice. Knowing where your boundaries lie and what they represent is essential if you are to have a strong sense of your masculine power.

Awareness of Death

The Warrior is always aware of the possibility of his own death. Robert Moore and Douglas Gillette made the point that many Warrior traditions believe the Warrior's clarity of thought is a quality he possesses because he's constantly aware of the imminence of his own death.

They suggested a Warrior is well aware of the shortness of life and how fragile it is. They believed this awareness can promote an outpouring of the life force and create an experience of life so intense that others can only imagine what this might be like.

Imagine the mind-set of male warriors of the American Native People going into battle with the cry "Today is a good day to die!" ringing in their ears. What an intensity of experience! Every moment of life would be fully lived. Maybe that is what we seek when we say "Live every day as though you might die tomorrow."

Such intensity suggests the true Warrior will not hesitate in his actions. And indeed, a man who is acting in this way, with every move guided by clear decisions and focused action, should certainly be able to engage with life fully.

Perhaps this aspect of the Warrior's psyche is the origin of the expression "He who hesitates is lost", meaning that it's often better to make a decision and stick to it than to change your mind. Thinking too much in a crisis can lead to hesitation. And hesitation can lead to the ultimate failure as a Warrior – losing the battle.

To put it simply: to embody the qualities of the Warrior in his fullness you need to be able to make split-second decisions on which you can rely, and you then need to be able to act upon those decisions with force and certainty.

This level of efficiency can be achieved through training and practice. It's obvious that any outstanding Warrior in any area of life – the martial arts or other sporting disciplines, the armed forces, police service, fire brigade and so on – gains a large part of his power and potency from training.

Training for battle – any kind of battle, not just warfare – activates certain qualities within the Warrior's psyche. These include skill, self-control, accuracy, decisiveness, and above all the self-discipline needed not to crumble in the heat of battle, whether that battle be physical, emotional or spiritual.

A true Warrior will never act in a way that inflates his power in his own eyes; he will never try to convince himself that he is more than he actually is. A true Warrior knows his power, knows his potential, and is well aware of his potency. He brings these qualities to his battles in a disciplined, controlled and totally present state of mind. This state of mind is a characteristic of great achievers in any field.

Self-control

A Warrior's self-control is a form of self-discipline which embraces persistence in the face of setback, complete belief and positivity about the outcome of whatever tasks need to be completed, and the capacity to withstand emotional and physical pain. There is no room for self-doubt in a true Warrior.

To the extent that we embody this self-control so we can develop Warrior energy. While all jobs need at least some Warrior energy simply to get things done, if your chosen job needs a lot of Warrior energy – such as salesman, fire-fighter, police officer, teacher, doctor, lawyer, builder, miner, nurse and so on – then you also need a lot of self-control.

This self-control is something every one of us who has embarked on a journey in life which requires endurance, persistence, resilience and determination knows about. The more you have it, the stronger the Warrior archetype within you. When you understand this, you also understand how discipline of mind and body are essential for the achievement of your goals.

A Set Of Principles

I've already described how the archetypal Warrior is no mindless servant. He has discernment and uses it to ensure that the cause for which he is fighting is a just and noble one.

Does this mean, you might ask, that soldiers who fight for tyrannical and repressive regimes are not true Warriors? Were the soldiers who supported Hitler or any of the other tyrants in human history mere puppets of those tyrannical regimes rather than true Warriors?

In one sense this must be true. These men, like many before them, fought more or less willingly for tyrants, bullies and immature leaders.

If an immature leader is to wage war and win he must gather around him Warriors who lack discernment and who are prepared to follow orders blindly. In fact, in modern warfare such blind obedience is often necessary. Soldiers may not have a choice about fighting. Troops may not really be aware of the bigger issues behind conflicts, especially when they are puppet soldiers dancing to a tyrant's tune. But even though soldiers may not be informed about the cause for which they are dying, there is no reason for us to follow their example.

Each and every one of us fighting our own battles, of whatever kind, can choose to make clear, principled decisions for ourselves. In our own lives we can decide what is sufficiently noble and sufficiently in line with our deepest values to be worth fighting for.

For example, are the ethics and morality of the company for which you work in line with your deepest values? If not, are you prepared to find a company for whom you can work with integrity? Are you doing what is right by your family, defending them against dangers of all kinds in a way that matches your principles? Do you treat your employees and associates with clean warrior energy or a barely concealed form of vindictive bullying?

You get the idea, I'm sure.

This is the important point here: citizens of a country may be pressed into service in the Armed Forces whether they like it or not. However, those of us who have causes and principles for which we are prepared to fight can make our own choices and decisions about the rightness of what we are doing.

Within the context of that idea, now take a moment to answer these two possibly uncomfortable questions before you read on: what cause, what values, what principle, would *you* be prepared to die for? To put it another way, what do you believe in so clearly and with such passion that you would be willing to fight to the death to defend it?

When we explore the male archetypes in my workshops I ask men what they would be prepared to die for. The answer I get most frequently is "my children" or "my family". Perhaps that is an example of warrior energy manifesting in its purest and most mature masculine form. In fact, nowhere is this clearer than in men who have just had children. Even when I simply ask these men to *imagine* a threat to their infants they usually experience a wild rush of protective warrior energy that seems to come from the core of their being. I haven't met a man yet for whom this was not true. You may have felt this yourself.

You probably understand that the quality of the Warrior's loyalty and the way in which he conducts himself are associated with something greater than him. This may be a cause, a set of values, or some principle. It is always something which is just and worthy of the Warrior's investment of commitment, time and energy. Yet how, in our society today, is a man to find a cause which his Warrior can justifiably serve? As you may expect, the answer to this question is often provided by your King, your Sovereign archetype. One of your Sovereign's most important roles is to help you find the truest expression of all parts of yourself, including your Warrior.

Emotional Detachment

Sometimes an ordinary man may have to step out of his humanity and stop feeling human emotion to fulfil his role as a Warrior. After the Second World War, a military historian named Colonel Sam Marshall claimed that he'd interviewed hundreds of troops after they'd been in battle. He also claimed his work showed that only a minority of enlisted US troops would knowingly fire on the enemy – between fifteen and thirty percent.

This myth has been repeated many times since then, for all kinds of reasons. Sometimes, perhaps, because we'd like to believe that we are innately caring and well-disposed towards our fellow man, and sometimes to show that killing does not come naturally to us.

However, Marshall got it wrong. The reality of conscripted soldiers' conduct in battle was very different. Fredric Smoler has written a fascinating account of a detailed investigation by a later military historian named Roger Spiller into Marshall's claims. Smoler shows us the uncomfortable truth. He concludes: "In battle's hard school, ordinary people eventually discover, quite by themselves, the knack of skilful killing."

In short, ordinary men and women can indeed become killers.

Often the transition between "ordinary men and women" and trained killer seems to be a very short step. You may say that any one of us could make the step into killing another human being, given a powerful enough reason, ranging from political indoctrination to an obvious threat to our homeland, loved ones, and ourselves. And that's precisely the point – the inhumane detached killer in us seems to lie not far beneath the surface.

For many men – and in our age women – this killing is most obvious in war. But even though the human transition to killer seems to come easily, this does not necessarily mean that a Warrior is cruel. It may simply mean that a Warrior is making his decisions in a detached way that best serves the greater need for which he is fighting. (Although, as we all know, sadistic and inhumane killers do exist.)

Of course in any battle, warfare or not, there may be a stepping away from emotion. Sometimes there is no choice but to put feeling aside. This ability to detach from feeling is part of what enables rescue workers such as firemen to enter burning buildings and save people's lives at the risk of their own.

And emotional detachment can be helpful to all of us. When the Warrior has to act in service of the greater good, for example by killing what needs to end, such as a relationship which has outgrown its time, emotional detachment allows a cleaner and easier severing of connection. Later, other parts of us can grieve the loss.

Destruction and Renewal

Running right through any discussion of the Warrior archetype is our awareness of the destruction this archetype can bring about. But to look at the inhumane destruction of modern warfare, say, and be deceived into thinking that such destruction is an inevitable part of the Warrior's way of doing things is a mistake.

A Warrior in his highest purpose will destroy only that which needs to be destroyed so that something new and more virtuous can take its place.

This may mean the end of a relationship, or a change of lifestyle, or standing up for what you believe in, or something else. This is the Warrior responding to the "No!" we may feel in our guts, the "No!" which tells us enough is enough, but which so many of us can and do ignore.

To kill that which needs to die is a true Warrior virtue.

You only need to look around the world today to see many things which you might well think need to be destroyed and replaced by something better, including evil and despotic governments. In fact you may think there are plenty of places where using warrior energy to destroy these harmful entities would indeed be a just and right mission. Yet that view discounts the pain and suffering of the people who would be harmed if the Warrior were to act. Our own feelings about such destruction, and our empathy for those who would be hurt, is held in another part of us – our Lover archetype.

You may be able to accept that Warriors sometimes need to kill or destroy what currently exists in order for something new to take its place. But for such "killing" to be beneficial there must also be a powerful Sovereign with a strong enough vision, and enough power, to ensure that what has been destroyed is replaced with something more wholesome.

The Warrior and Other Archetypes

The Warrior archetype needs to work in harmony with other archetypes, for warrior energy working alone can be uncontrolled and potentially very destructive. Yet when the Warrior works for the Sovereign, together they create an energy from which something truly magnificent can emerge.

Many of our greatest films, legends, books and other stories depict the mature King and the mature Warrior acting together to produce profound change where it is needed. Sometimes these energies are found within the same individual, a man we can truly call a Warrior King.

To take this idea further, when your Warrior's fierceness is tempered by the authority and judgement of your Sovereign and guided by the wisdom of your Magician, you can be a truly inspiring force in the world. You can get things done!

Indeed, a true Warrior King can guide family, corporations and even countries into greater prosperity through his committed and discerning stewardship of the Kingdom – and his fearless action on its behalf.

Of course the Warrior can also connect with the Lover archetype to bring an awareness of the interconnectedness that all living things have with each other and with planet Earth. When he touches his Lover, a Warrior may come back into connection with his humanity. He is reminded that those he may have to destroy in some way (whether that be physically, emotionally or spiritually) are just like him: thinking, feeling, sensitive human beings.

So a Warrior can be compassionate. But this quality will only be manifested in his actions when he is connected to his Lover energy. Without such restraint, such softening, the actions of the Warrior can be truly disastrous both for the Warrior himself and for the world around him.

Uncontrolled by his King, free of the tempering influence of his Lover, and without the counsel of his Magician, a Warrior may run amok, careless of consequence, driven by self-interest. In his purest form he may pillage and destroy to get what he wants, then rejoice in the plunder, ravage his rewards, and cast them aside without a second thought. This is why all Warriors need a King who can control them.

Your Warrior Needs To Serve You

For some men with strong warrior energy, the welfare of even those closest to them comes second to the pursuit of the battles in their lives. And no wonder. To achieve success in anything which requires the Warrior archetype to go out and "win" is immensely self-affirming for men. This is, after all, a core archetype in the male psyche.

Do you doubt it? Then pause to consider for a moment – which is more important to you: your work or your relationship with your wife or partner? Staying with your family or finding your place in the world of men?

So many men hesitate to answer those questions truthfully. Deep down, they know that success in life, even in small matters, as well as getting things done in their world, is what really matters to them. For some, victory on what they see as the "battlefield" of life is most important. No surprise, then, that champion sportsmen have elevated levels of testosterone after winning. The expression of this competitive energy, an energy deeply programmed within our male genes, brings each of us more fully into a sense of who we are as men. After all, is anything more important than winning, at least to a Warrior?

Whatever your own truth around warrior energy, none of us is served by trying to hide, repress or deny the Warrior archetype within us. Rather, what is required of each of us is that we manage our Warrior so he serves us, and everyone around us, most usefully.

For some men I've worked with this means focusing the Warrior by training in martial arts. For others it means adopting a very focused attitude to business. For others it means finding a cause, a set of values, or a purpose which is personally important and which can be embraced with whole-heartedness.

For some it means protecting the family and doing everything necessary to ensure the family's well-being. For others it is about fighting for justice. For many men, it is about forging a path of their own choosing through life. But whatever it means for you, there's no question that your powerful Warrior needs to be carefully managed and harnessed in the service of your Sovereign rather than allowed to rampage around on his own account. This is explained more fully in the chapter on the Sovereign.

Anger, Fear and Weakness

From time to time I work in an organization which runs weekend workshops designed to bring men to a fuller, closer relationship with their mature masculinity and maleness. One of the objectives we have is to help them embody their Warrior archetype in a healthy way.

When men arrive for their weekend on Friday evening, I see a lot of fear.

Yet when I talk to men who were doing this work 20 years ago, they tell me that most of the men in those days arrived with a lot of anger. This seeming shift from anger towards fear might be a reflection of society's fear of masculine warrior energy. This has probably not been helped by a feminist movement against male authoritarianism and the power of the patriarchy.

I believe some men have internalized this energy as self-hatred or fear of their own masculinity. Now they simply don't have access to clean male energy. Rather, they look like the "new men" of our time – incomplete, eager to please, emotionally immature, living in fear of the feminine and fearing their own male power.

Yet this is not their fault. Not really. After all, who is there in society to teach young men how to become powerful adult men with easy access to their warrior energy?

Traditionally this would have been the job of the Elders and adult men in the village, who would put the boy through a series of more or less terrifying initiation rituals which might result in his death. This process was designed to transform his fear into warrior power so that he could fully live his destiny as a Warrior.

Nowadays, although we need warrior energy just as much to survive the demands and rigours of our modern technological society and all its challenges, most men are not introduced to their Warrior archetype in any meaningful way. In fact for many men warrior energy is completely repressed into the shadow unconscious.

And even in shadow this warrior energy (which you can call male energy, assertiveness, the energy of action in the world, anger, aggressiveness and no doubt many other names) retains its power. It will emerge sooner or later as the Warrior's shadows – uncontrolled and destructive.

The Emotional Wound In The Warrior Quarter

We think of the Warrior archetype as the source of the masculine energy responsible for getting things done in the world. And so it is, but underlying this is a deeper need in all of us to make an impact on the world.

To make an impact you must be sure at the heart of your being that your very existence is right and proper. You must know you have a right to exist, a right to occupy the space you're in. And an unconditional right at that.

And to know that, you must know where your physical and emotional boundaries lie. You must have a clear sense of your own identity. Only then will you be able to build the foundations of true adult male power and presence, and have the ability to make an impact on others.

In an ideal world these qualities emerge naturally as a child grows and develops. When a baby is born there is no separation in the baby's mind between baby and mother. That separation develops over the first year of life as the child gradually comes to realize that he or she is a separate being with the ability to impact the world and get his or her needs met. This is part of the child's identity formation and individuation.

At the same time as he starts to develop an awareness of his psychological boundaries, he also naturally begins to experience the boundaries of his body. These represent the physical boundaries of his existence in the world.

If all goes well with this process a child will develop a clear sense of separation from his parents. As he does so, he gradually realizes he can make demands of the world and comes to understand he can refuse to cooperate with the demands made of him. He realizes he has a will of his own and that he can say "No!" And so he comes to understand he has power in the world.

Very often a child's "No" is more about learning to set boundaries than saying "I don't want that!" In reality the child is exploring the difference, the separation, between himself and his parents. At the same time he is experimenting with his newly discovered sense of power and potency in the world.

If his parents are strong enough, mature enough, and wise enough to hold this energy in a loving way and to accept their child's "No!" as a sign of his individuality and growth, then he can develop a strong sense of self-identity and come to know he has power in the world.

This is a healthy process which leads a child to the unconscious certainty that he is indeed his own person and that he has a right to exist in the world in his own image. And then he can naturally embrace many of the qualities of the balanced Warrior.

Unfortunately ours is not an ideal world.

A lot of men in my men's Emotional Process Work workshops tell me how their mothers, fathers, siblings, friends and other adults invaded their boundaries when they were children.

In fact I think almost every child experiences adults infringing their boundaries in one way or another. That can range from a lack of respect for their privacy or personal space all the way through to deliberate emotional, physical or sexual abuse.

But whether minor or major, any kind of boundary incursion, repeated often enough, inevitably has some impact on a child's developing identity, sense of self and warrior energy. And each time it happens the response inside the child is likely to be anger. That's because anger is not only the energy which *drives* boundary setting; it is also the natural *response* to the infringement of our boundaries.

Unfortunately anger is an emotion which can be difficult for parents to accept in their child. Some parents have their own issues with anger. Maybe it scares them. Maybe they can't hold it safely for their child while he learns to hold it safely for himself. Maybe they just don't want an angry child in the family.

Whatever the reason, a child may have to repress his anger if he is to be accepted as a full member of the family unit. This is a direct assault on the child's right to express his feelings freely. It's also an assault on his right to an independent, individuated existence.

The message which the child picks up is some variation of "You can't exist as a separate person in your own right." More simply, we could express the message as "Don't exist as you are."

Of course the Warrior wound doesn't have to be as extreme as an overt or covert injunction which says "Don't exist." Often the message a child picks up is something more like "You can't be yourself." "You can't exist as who you are." "You are only wanted here if you become what we want you to be." And so on.

These are messages which tell the child his existence in the world will always be conditional on him being a certain way, or on getting somebody else's approval. And that can be just as harmful to a child's sense of self as the simpler and more direct message "Don't exist."

So the Warrior wound is an emotional wound about existence and identity. Somehow a child comes to understand that his identity, the way he is, perhaps even his very existence, simply isn't acceptable in its natural form. Somehow he comes to know that his right to assert himself, his natural self-confidence, his assertiveness, and even the anger which arises when his boundaries are infringed cannot be freely expressed. Instead it must be put into shadow. This is an emotional wounding which can have devastating consequences.

There are many variations of this wounding which can continue throughout boyhood and adolescence. For example, if a boy's tears are unacceptable to his family, the message the child receives may be something like: "We don't want your sadness around here. Take it somewhere else. If you want to be a part of this family, don't show your sadness to us."

When faced with this ultimatum, whether it's spoken or implicit, a boy will repress his tears because he wants to remain a part of the family group both physically and emotionally. He may start to cover his tears and sadness by hiding them behind anger. (I've met many men in the course of my work who weren't allowed to express their anger during childhood and put it into shadow to please their parents. I've met many more who did not have the freedom to show their grief and so put their sadness and tears into shadow.)

Whatever the exact nature of his wounding, if a boy learns to hide, repress and deny the anger which naturally arises in him when his boundaries are violated, he will develop a relationship with anger which definitely won't serve him later in life.

He may not be able to assert himself. He may not know what is acceptable to him and what isn't. He may not be able to say "No!" He may be called names like "pussy" or "wimp". He may feel like a walk-over. In the extreme he may become a boundary-less individual who is open to invasion from everyone who wants to step over his boundaries, deliberately or accidentally. He may become passive-aggressive, showing indirect resistance to the demands of others and an avoidance of direct confrontation.

There can be more subtle consequences as well. If a boy doesn't develop an appropriate level of self-confidence, assertiveness and warrior energy, and the well-defined sense of self that goes with it, as an adult he may simply not know what he stands for. One minute he'll agree with one person, one point of view, and the next he'll agree with somebody else taking precisely the opposite point of view.

In short, the more a boy represses his anger the less likely he is to become a man able to defend his boundaries, stand up for himself, speak his mind forcefully, take appropriate action, be powerful and decisive, and generally make a mark in the world.

Of course the energy of anger repressed into shadow does not go away. Often it builds up bit by bit until it reaches cyclone-like force. Then, perhaps in response to the slightest trigger, this energy may erupt as emotional or physical violence all over anyone or anything unfortunate enough to be near the man. In the opposite extreme, the suppressed anger is turned against the self and becomes some kind of reactive depression.

But whether his anger inflates (intensifies) or deflates (becomes less obvious), its energy is alive and well inside the man's shadow unconscious, from where it will constantly leak out in various ways. The Warrior's shadows can indeed be frightening. Let's look at them in more detail.

The Warrior's Shadows

When you think about the explosions of rage and the cruelty and brutality which men and women can display, you might wonder how human beings can be capable of such depravity and lack of feeling. The answer lies in the almost unimaginable power of the Shadow Warrior.

Every archetypal shadow has two opposing poles known as the inflated and the deflated form. The Warrior's shadow can manifest in the inflated form of the Sadist or Bully, and in the deflated form of the Masochist, victim, or coward.

The Inflated Shadow: The Bully, Sadist or Perpetrator

Once warrior energy goes into shadow, it may inflate – in other words grow. Robert Moore and Douglas Gillette called the inflated Shadow Warrior the "Sadist". Another word is "Bully". It's an energy which takes many forms.

Inflation of shadow warrior anger can produce a man who is volatile, unpredictable, and who oozes aggression out of every pore. This is the man around whom no-one feels safe. He looks like he might explode at any moment.

And indeed he might, most commonly in outbursts of rage provoked by something quite trivial. Road rage is a well known example of this. This kind of male shadow anger is often directed against other people, which is why it can be so dangerous. Women in particular know this.

Sometimes the Warrior wound can lead to failure to form a clear self-identity, so men with a strong Shadow Warrior may try to affirm some kind of identity for themselves by joining a particular group and labelling themselves with the identity of the group. We see that in the case of gangs, religious institutions, members of the military, and so on.

Another aspect of this weak identity is the way some men seek to "big" themselves up by wearing "big name brands" and buying products with so-called designer labels. This feels phony and has the air of someone desperately shouting "Look who I am! I am someone of significance!"

Another sign of the inflation of warrior energy is seen in the man who constantly asserts himself, trying to be bigger than he really is, threatening others, taking offence at the slightest hint of an insult, and generally "looking for trouble".

Another common example of the inflated Warrior is to be found in the increasingly recognized experience of workplace bullying.

Most often shadow anger manifests in the form of the sadistic Warrior or bully. If a man allows this Shadow Warrior to outwardly express his desire for destruction and cruelty, he may feel some kind of satisfaction and perhaps even pleasure as he torments his victims.

This sadism, bullying, taunting and victimization can sit alongside a hatred of those whom the Shadow Warrior perceives as weak and on whom he perpetrates his violence. (Of course, this behaviour is all about denying the fact that the man himself is a weak Warrior.)

The Shadow Warrior is insecure, adolescent in outlook, and violently emotional. Yet, strangely, these qualities mirror aspects of the Hero archetype, the boyhood form of the Warrior archetype.

Robert Moore and Douglas Gillette saw the Hero as an energetic archetype which provides an adolescent boy with the energy to break free from the feminine, both internally and externally, so he can identify with, and join, the world of the masculine. In their view, men under the control of the Shadow Warrior who behave like sadists are unsure of their legitimate male power. In fact they suggested that an inflated Warrior, like an adolescent boy, might still be waging war against the power of his inner feminine or "Anima". It's certainly possible. Either way, we'll look more closely at the energy of the Hero in a moment.

The more you look around our society, the more you can spot the inflated Shadow Warrior in one form or another. He manifests as the wife-beater, the teenage bully, the abusive father, the unreasonable, harassing boss or bullying co-worker, even the rapist, and so on.

One thing which can really activate the Sadist or Bully is the sight of weakness. When a man's Shadow Warrior sees weakness – whether that is part of a man's own psyche or something in the world around him – he may charge out of hiding and start wielding his sword with ridiculous violence and power, metaphorically chopping off the heads of everyone within reach.

In other words, the sadistic Shadow Warrior's victim can just as easily be the man in whom he resides as anyone else. When he turns against his host, some form of self-harming behaviour pattern is a common result. One common expression of this may be the self-driven workaholic who seems to have no time for himself.

This is the energy we see in managers who stay on at work after everyone else has gone home. We see it in therapists, social workers, doctors and nurses who endlessly try to meet the needs of other people's emotional well-being, even at the expense of their own.

In short, these are people who don't care for themselves. They act out the drive of the Shadow Warrior under the guise of helping others or saving the world, while simultaneously harming themselves and perhaps their families as well. Although subtler and more refined than the energy of the outright bully, this still seems to be the energy of the Shadow Warrior, this time turned against the self.

In reality, if a man doesn't have an internal psychological structure strong enough to withstand the force of his Shadow Warrior, any situation which puts a great deal of pressure on him can empower the Shadow Warrior to take control.

I saw this in a young father in his twenties who attended one of my workshops. He was having trouble with his anger – well, rage really – towards his young children.

As a child he had suffered at the hands of his own violent father. Unsurprisingly, he had internalized his father's rage and abusiveness. Now under relentless pressure as family breadwinner and father of three young boys he could not control his anger, particularly during the stressful periods in his life.

He found himself overtaken in an instant by the energy of his Shadow Warrior, who raged abusively and violently, unexpectedly and uncontrollably. No matter how much he wanted to do things differently, he seemed unable to change his behaviour.

By allowing him to express this part of himself fully and without restriction, in symbolic form and in a safe setting, we were able to get the anger out of shadow and more integrated into his conscious awareness. This gave him much greater control over his rage and allowed him to start responding, rather than instantly reacting, to situations which had previously triggered his Shadow Warrior.

The Deflated Shadow: The Masochist, Coward or Victim

The deflated Shadow Warrior, the one who tends not to show any anger, may be a masochist, coward, weakling or victim. Repressed anger directed against the self can also manifest as a form of chronic depression or lack of motivation.

The masochist may feel like a doormat, a mummy's boy, a wimp. It's the quality which can evoke the abusive insult "Don't be such a pussy!" These words refer to the passivity and lack of power or presence in this expression of the Warrior's shadow.

And just like the Sadist, this shadow originates in some kind of alienation from healthy, balanced warrior energy.

Maybe a man in the grip of the weak Shadow Warrior never learned how to be a man. Perhaps his father was absent. Perhaps his mother was invasive. Perhaps he was bullied mercilessly by older siblings while he was growing up. Somehow his power was taken away from him, that's for sure.

Whatever the cause, a man's move into the weakling Masochist renders him unable to defend himself psychologically or physically. Others are able to walk all over him. Weakling, wimp, coward, pussy, call this shadow what you will, it is a distinctive archetype where a man has no boundaries. He does not know what he stands for, or even where he stands.

He may allow others to push him beyond the limits of his tolerance, sometimes to the point where the repressed energy of his Warrior erupts as rage. His rage, when it comes, is usually expressed by breaking inanimate objects, not people.

Men in this situation may accept what is unacceptable in ways that astound those around them. They have few boundaries or clear opinions of their own. They are swayed by the opinions and actions of others. They are weak and easily influenced by the tyrannical and abusive, whom they may gladly serve. After all, if they cannot set their own boundaries they can at least conform to someone else's. They can get a taste of power by standing in the reflection of another's tyranny.

The deflation of anger in shadow can look like passivity and indecisiveness. It may lead to a man's inability to decide what he stands for, or his inability to resist the invasion of his emotional or physical boundaries by other people. And since anger is simply one expression of the most basic masculine energy, a repression of anger into shadow is naturally linked to an absence of the energy to get anything done in the real world.

There's often an inability to stand up to the feminine, too. This man may be unable to stand firm in the face of his woman's anger and incapable of providing her with the clear, firm boundaries that would make her feel safe.

Deflated anger can also appear as depression, anger turned against the self. No wonder, really, because the Warrior who sees no hope or possibility of going out into the world and having any impact on anything may well feel pointless, hopeless and even self-destructive.

In fact I suspect many suicides come from a deep wound in the Warrior quarter, from either an absence of clear self-identity or a profound sense of having no real right to exist. The inability to make any kind of impact on the world must be a devastating blow to a man's self-esteem. It's not hard to see how this might be linked with suicide. If you don't have any sense of having the right to occupy the space you're in, well, why would you value your life very highly?

A man with a weak Warrior archetype often projects his own warrior energy out onto those around him and accepts the bullying or tyranny of others willingly because it represents some twisted form of safety and certainty. Rather than set his own boundaries he absorbs the Warrior power of those around him. This is a man who stands for nothing and falls for everything.

Yet although he has little mastery of either his own boundaries or his own warrior energy, the Masochist or weakling may switch polarities into the Sadist or bully without warning. This is the source of the unexpected eruption of rage or violence in a man who has been pushed beyond his limits.

By contrast, the mature, balanced Warrior archetype is a state of mind achieved by discipline and the practice of self-control. This healthy Warrior archetype lives under the direction of the Sovereign archetype, the King who is in control and running the show.

You see, your Sovereign is – or at least should be – the part of your psychological and emotional system which issues orders to your Warrior, keeps him in check, ensures that his needs are met, and gives him constructive and purposeful projects to fulfil.

I've noticed that without such attention and support Warriors tend to find a way of doing their own thing, usually to the detriment of the men in whom they reside. In fact, in such circumstances they often create chaos. Are you experiencing the chaos of an out-of-control Warrior in your life?

If you pause and look around your inner world for a moment, how is your Warrior doing? More to the point, perhaps, *what* is he doing?

Is he running amok, doing his own thing without the control, restriction or influence of your Sovereign? Is he rampaging around the boundaries of your Kingdom with no clear purpose? Or is he invading other people's territory and space without regard for their feelings or boundaries? Is he trying to start a war?

Or is your Warrior passive, resigned, feeling abandoned and unwanted, sitting idly somewhere in your Kingdom waiting for orders or even attention from your King? And leaving you feeling demotivated, deactivated, de-energized and lacking in any sense of achievement, power and purpose?

A final thought on the repression of anger: sometimes you may meet a man (or woman) who seems too nice to be true. Often you sense that something is missing from their personality. It feels like you are dealing with someone who has a part of them missing. And often they do – their anger, which is totally repressed, replaced by niceness and perhaps a kind of charming yet manipulative ability to get what they want or need through being agreeable and pleasant. This may be a person whose anger or assertiveness is deeply in shadow, lodged in the darkest recesses of the far corners of their shadow bag.

How To Be A Powerful Warrior

No matter what your Warrior is like right now, no matter what kind of relationship you have with him, you can make it better. You can develop a healthy, mature Warrior – a Warrior in his fullness.

1 Make Friends With Your Anger

A lot of men in the world now seem to be afraid of their anger and hide it behind their fear. Other men hide their anger behind their sadness, so their tears flow more easily than their anger.

Your experience in childhood made you the person you are now, but you certainly don't have to stay the same way for the rest of your life. If you really want to embody the full power of your mature masculinity you easily can bring your Warrior online.

If you have a problem with "uncontrollable" or excessive anger, find a workshop where you can get that anger out of shadow and integrate it. (See the resources section of the book for more ideas.) Your work may be to learn how to integrate your raging Shadow Warrior and become its master. That way you will no longer be controlled by the forces of your unconscious.

If you have a problem with too little anger, find a facilitator or coach who works with these archetypal energies and can help you discover what it means to feel the true energy of your balanced Warrior. You can also ask for help in overcoming your fears about expressing anger.

You may find it helpful to experience your own anger in the safe setting of a workshop where you can see other men model healthy anger which is under their conscious control. As you step more confidently into your own Warrior, you will gain more experience of your masculine power and begin to recover the energy of the man you really are.

Most importantly, make the decision to do something about your unbalanced Warrior energy from a place of Sovereignty or Kingship. After all, your King is the one who should be setting the strategy in your Kingdom. You can do this by symbolically stepping into your Sovereign in your imagination and then giving clear orders to your Warrior so he can go out and make what you want to have happen, happen. This is also something you can practice in a workshop setting.

In one of my recent workshops I asked a man deficient in Warrior energy to symbolically defend "his" territory in the centre of the room by stopping other men coming into that space. He had to do this with only the power of a hand gesture and the word "Stop!" This soon revealed his lack of warrior energy: men were all over his space! He seemed impotent to stop them.

This was a dramatic illustration of how some men can hardly find their genuine Warrior energy. Yet after he'd practiced this for a few minutes something remarkable happened: he began to clearly channel warrior energy in a powerful and balanced way.

Suddenly men stopped invading his space. They seemed to feel his Warrior, and their own internal Warriors instinctively knew not to mess with his boundaries. Of course, his next challenge was to take his Warrior into the world outside our workshop and do the same thing there.

All of this is about "making friends with your anger". That may mean coming to terms with the reality that you're a man and your genetic code is programmed so you feel anger when people infringe your boundaries.

You may also need to accept a harder reality: inside you there is a very ancient hunter-killer. The survival of the tribe once depended on him and his fellow Warriors. Most likely he is never going to be required to do the work of killing. So he needs something else to do; he needs to be a different kind of Warrior – one who gets things done in the world. A modern day Warrior.

To sum this up, your anger can manifest however you choose: consciously or unconsciously; in or out of shadow; under your control or out of your control. As genuine masculine power and force; as rage; as impotence; as anger turned against yourself in the form of depression. Decide how you want your anger to show up, and then find a way of making this happen under your control.

2 Control Your Rage

It's a mistake to think of male rage as a form of anger that's appropriate to the Warrior archetype. It is not.

There's a story about a Samurai warrior who went out to fight an enemy. As the Samurai drew his sword ready for battle the enemy spat on him. The Samurai sheathed his sword and walked away. Why?

Because in the moment when his enemy spat on him the Samurai felt rage. Knowing that if he killed his opponent in rage he would not be acting from the place of the Warrior's self-discipline, he chose not to act at all.

Unlike the Samurai warrior in this story, most men who have rage in their shadow have little or no control over how it emerges. They cannot stop it spilling out over family, friends, innocent passers-by, themselves and inanimate objects.

Some world "leaders" even seem to express their shadow rage by having their armies vicariously act it out by waging ridiculous wars against foreign countries few people have even heard about until those countries are catastrophically wrecked and millions of innocent men, women and children have died.

A simple truth: as men we carry a lot of unexpressed rage inside our bodies. Many of us are barely in connection with this rage, but it can all too easily leak out in verbal, emotional or physical aggression and even violence. This rage is the accumulation of huge amounts of unexpressed male energy – call it anger or aggression if you prefer.

This is the energy you feel but don't or can't express when you fail to stop people invading your boundaries. It's the energy you feel but don't express when others infringe your boundaries and you don't protect them. It's the unexpressed energy which arises in you when you're faced with threats to your territory or your possessions or something else important to you, and you do nothing about it.

And of course there is a deep part of you which wants to react to these things with violence. This is the instinctual male way: to respond with force to threat and a lack of respect for our boundaries. The problem is, no-one ever taught us how to handle our anger. We were never initiated into manhood in a way that gave us this knowledge and ability. Most of us never had a father who could show us how to control our anger, because our fathers were never taught these things either.

Surely, you don't deny this urge exists in you?

Over the years many men have told me they never dreamed they were capable of hitting their kids until they found their hand up in the air, ready to strike. They were all surprised and shocked by this. Many other men have told me how they have struck out in rage, either against other people, or by breaking objects to smithereens.

Michael, a highly successful businessman who came on one of my workshops to work on his anger towards his mother, told me how he'd smashed an entire set of bedroom furniture to pieces in a rage. He'd used a heavy table leg to vent his fury after an argument with his girlfriend in which she had innocently "triggered" him. She had somehow "become" his mother during the argument, after which the rest was predictable... fortunately she was not the physical target of his rage, but I guess he had to buy some new furniture afterwards.

After such an event there can be shame or guilt, a sense of relief or release, tears or fears. Such catharsis can in fact be very helpful in reducing your internal tension. But carrying this level of rage isn't good for anyone, least of all those around you. And what if you don't know you're carrying it?

What isn't expressed is repressed, and it builds up in the body. So if you're carrying the accumulated energy of a million little invasions of your boundaries throughout your life in situations where you could not or did not know how to respond, then you have a responsibility to find a way of releasing it – before it releases itself.

And that's not just by playing video games or watching violent films. These play into the Warrior archetype in a powerful way; I imagine that's why we find the vicarious representation of violence on TV and in the movies so compulsively engaging.

In real life, however, what you need is a place where you can be physically active. A place where you can break, smash, pound, chop, beat, sweat, grunt, feel your strength, howl, break things, throw heavy things about, smash other things, do whatever you need to do, and shout and swear the obscenities you need to express. In short, you need to have a place where you can do anything and everything simply to get this energy out of your system.

And remember this energy needs vocalizing. It's the scream of the Warrior on a killing rampage inside you trying to make itself heard.

What of those moments where you feel rage coming up? If you have no other recourse, simply drop to the floor and do between 10 and 30 push-ups as hard and fast as you can. See how that makes you feel. (Better, I hope!)

No matter where this potentially violent male warrior energy lives in your body, it needs to be under your control. That means every so often you need to find a space where you can let it out as much as possible, without inhibition, and as loudly as need be, in a safe way.

This approach to Warrior management prevents attacks on your co-workers, kids, wife or friends, stops passive-aggressive behaviours, avoids self-destructive internalized rage, and helps to prevent physical violence.

But to fully integrate your masculinity into your being you need to treat your internal primal spear-throwing hunter-killer with respect. You need to give him something to do that serves you in today's world. Most likely he cannot go out hunting for food, and he may not be needed to protect your family from warmongers from another tribe, but he still needs something to do, something which serves you in the world today.

To be fully integrated, you need to accept this energy as a part of you and contain it safely. That means expressing it often enough that it does not build up to dangerous levels. People know not to mess with you when it's safely contained. Your energy is strong but not threatening. It's an embodied energy that makes women and children and vulnerable people feel safe with you. They feel safe because they know you can – and will – protect them if necessary.

What do you need to do, right now, to make this happen for you?

3 Find A Physical Outlet That Matches Your Warrior's Needs

You may not want to take up a martial art, although it's highly recommended for developing the discipline of your inner Warrior.

But you might want to do something else physical: take part in contact sports, or wrestling, or maybe take up some kind of sport which is physically demanding and perhaps has an edge of danger – rock climbing, surfing, parachuting, that kind of thing. Try something that challenges you in a way you've never been challenged before, something which makes your blood pump so much you feel the Warrior inside you stirring as he remembers the archetypal energy that brought him into being.

And don't be a wimp about this. A wimp is a man who's disowned his Warrior and is acting weak or like a coward. You don't need to do anything dangerous; you just need to find a way to express and embody your masculine strength in all ways – physical, emotional and spiritual.

On a different front, if you're not moving forward with a vision for your life or if you're not taking action in the world to get what you want, then one of two things is probably wrong.

First, either your Sovereign doesn't have a vision that's powerful enough to motivate him to give orders to your Warrior. Or second, your Warrior isn't powerful enough to go out into the world and get shit done.

Stop being weak, acting like a wimp, a pushover or a coward, and start being a King and a Warrior. This means forming a vision, living your mission, knowing your purpose, setting your goals, having an intention for every day of your life, and using your masculine power to actually bring these things into your life. If you don't know how to do that, find a man who can teach you.

4 Stop Being Passive & Get Your Balls Back

Some of the men who come to my Emotional Process Workshops look like someone's taken their balls away. And strangely enough, that's exactly what *has* happened to many of them, metaphorically if not literally.

On the one hand their fathers were absent or simply couldn't show them how to be a man – not that their fathers had much idea about masculinity either. On the other hand they were over-attached to the world of the feminine (and continue so to be) because mother, sisters or some other feminine influence caught them and never let them go. These men, often soft and gentle, need help in embracing their masculinity.

Nothing represents male softness as clearly as the 1990s vogue of the "new man". This short-lived fashion was perhaps a response to feminism, whereby men – some men anyway – adapted to become what they thought women wanted of them: nice, sweet, sensitive, and somehow feminized. You may not be surprised to learn that women pretty quickly realized this wasn't what they wanted at all. They wanted men who were safe, protective, strong, and above all free of repressed anger and resentment towards women.

So getting your balls back is about giving up the feminine and embodying what we could call the sacred masculine on every level – emotional, physical, spiritual. It's about being strong in every part of your being. ("Sacred" simply meaning pure, ancient and ancestral, something to be honoured.)

The reality is that a man who's lost his balls is mild and non-assertive. He doesn't know what he stands for. He may agree with one person one minute, and someone with dramatically opposing views the next. Most likely he doesn't know how to stand up for himself against men or women. He may not have any clear opinions.

Maybe he's done lots of workshops about feeling and sensitivity – not that there's anything wrong with that, as long as it isn't all he's done by way of self-development. Maybe he's "deeply spiritual". Maybe his experience of self-development workshops extends no further than endless Tantra weekends – not that there's anything wrong with that, either... as long as it isn't all he's done.

In short, he's deficient in the solid core of masculinity which enables a man to go out into the world and make an impact in his own way. He doesn't really know what it means to be a man in the world. He may have some Warrior energy but somehow he isn't a full-blooded man. Everyone in his life has a stake in him. He isn't his own man.

This raises the question of how a boy becomes a man. A lot of it has to do with having dad around, or perhaps some other suitable male role models, so the boy can learn how men are in the world. But it also has to do with a boy being allowed to test himself in situations that allow him to develop his assertiveness, experience his capacity to impact the world, and fully feel (and where necessary control) his fear, his anger, and his courage.

A problem I see here is that rather a lot of women appear to be frightened of masculine energy in men and boys. They seem to fear men who are assertive and live their lives pushing the edge of what's possible for them. These women sometimes look like they're unconsciously trying to nullify male energy in their boys and their men. Perhaps they are afraid of male rage, perhaps with good reason. However, this situation does nobody any good, least of all the boys.

Men who live in a less-than-fully masculine way do themselves no favours because they don't experience the reality of who they are at their genetic core. And they do women no favours because as men they are simply not able to consciously and fully meet the feminine energy of their partners. I believe most women want a strong man who can set clear boundaries and protect them and their children, because then they can feel truly safe.

Such men harm their children too, by not showing their kids what true masculinity is all about. Bearing in mind that children learn most things about masculinity from their fathers, you can see how a passive man may inadvertently teach his sons a few things they don't need to know: how to be dominated by women, how to shrink from challenges, and how to weaken in the face of the hard knocks that life inevitably provides. So what to do about this?

First of all, the man has to work out who's got his balls. When he knows that, he has to symbolically and energetically get them back. Then he needs to find a place where other men can help him embody the essence of his new found masculinity on a day-to-day basis.

A powerful men's group is a great place to do those things, particularly if it's made up of men who understand the concepts of emotional intelligence, honesty, trust, accountability and integrity among men. (You might like to look into what the ManKind Project offers if this sounds interesting to you: www.mkp.org)

Mixing with the right kind of men in life also helps – that's men who don't shrink from a challenge, who live life to the full, and who know exactly who they are (or are on their way to finding out). And doing your own personal emotional work is important. There are plenty of men's workshops where men can extract feminine energy that's been injected into them through no fault of their own, and replace it with something more masculine.

5 Do Your Personal Work

One of the quickest and easiest ways to recover your masculinity is to plunge headfirst into your unconscious, root out the reprogramming that somebody else put in there, and replace it with a truly masculine program, one that will make you the man you were always meant to be. And the thing that counts here is *action*.

After 20 years' work in various fields of psychotherapy with both men and women, I believe one of the most powerful ways to achieve rapid personal change is to find a way to work with your archetypes and your unconscious Shadow. Your Shadow is made up of the thoughts, feelings and emotions you hide, repress and deny, both as child and adult.

Carl Jung showed us how the drivers behind our behaviour lie deep in our unconscious. For example, as a child you may have been told or shown or taught – directly or indirectly – that anger was not acceptable in your family environment. Or you might have picked up the message that your sexuality was shameful or even disgusting.

Whatever you were taught, you would surely have repressed all of the "unacceptable" aspects of yourself to keep the acceptance and maybe even the love of your family. But trying to close these feelings down, hide them, or repress them out of sight in the unconscious mind is a double-edged sword.

What you repressed as a child and what you repress now will not lose its power. Far from it: in fact the power of what is repressed gradually increases simply *because* it's not expressed.

The energy gradually grows, becoming more and more influential over your behaviour, disrupting your relationships, perhaps causing you to break down in unexpected grief, or to experience moments of rage. Sometimes it manifests as bodily symptoms, as aches and pains, as illness of one kind or another.

This is the nature of your shadow unconscious. Often the material which bursts out of shadow feels as if it is somehow "not part of you". It may feel like it is separate from you, has come from nowhere you know about, and has complete control over you.

The process of emotional healing starts in earnest when you take a decision to delve deep down into your unconscious and look at the emotional wounds you've experienced in each of your archetypes or sub-personalities: Warrior, Magician, Lover and King. Then you can start to heal the emotional wounds you've experienced and recover the essence of your masculinity in its pure, original and truly magnificent form.

For men who have somehow been "de-balled" this kind of work is absolutely essential if they're to recover their true masculinity and express it in their own lives.

And for anybody still wondering why this matters, it's simple: a life lived split off from your natural essence as a man feels empty, desolate, a shadow of a satisfying life. If you continue to live such a life, you may well die unhappy, unfulfilled, and full of regret and bitterness. There is a better way, and seeking it out is a choice that you can make right now: all you have to do is find the path in life that will take you on a journey to recover your masculinity.

6 Live with Integrity and Authenticity

Every man has his own values. Examples of values include loyalty, courage, strength, defending what's important, loving freely, trusting others, integrity and honesty.

You are the only one who can decide what your values are, but two stand out for me: integrity and authenticity. I think these values are two essential foundation stones of mature masculinity.

Yet to live a life of complete integrity is one of the hardest possible challenges for any man. From time to time we all take shortcuts, we all make life easy for ourselves, we all skip the difficult challenges. Life can be hard and sometimes it's just easier to turn the other cheek, tell a lie, hide from the truth, and avoid facing up to our responsibilities.

None of which, I might say, stops us developing a practice of building a little bit more integrity every day. But what exactly, you might respond, does it mean to be "in integrity" as a man?

In fact it's simple. Integrity means that you do what you say you will do, you are who you say you are, and your actions match your words. So integrity means you live in truth. You know you are responsible for the consequences of your actions, intended or unintended. You accept those responsibilities.

And of course to stay in integrity as a man you must keep your commitments, whether they are implicit or explicit. When you marry your wife you make an implicit commitment to be faithful to her – and you keep it. When you have children you enter into an implicit commitment with them to look after them. Hopefully you also make an explicit commitment *with yourself* to protect your children and be a great father to them. You keep those commitments. You do your best to fulfil all the other commitments and agreements you enter into. If for some reason you cannot, you find a way to make it up to those whom you have let down. And in all of that you continue to keep your commitments to yourself.

Authenticity and integrity also mean living by a set of values. For me these values include treating others decently, respecting women, looking after children, honouring planet Earth, and setting certain standards for my own behaviour, among other things.

When you embody qualities like this you are authentic: you are who you say you are and the world knows it. By staying in integrity in this way you forge a path to your own Sovereignty and become a role model for all those around you. You also become an example for other men who haven't yet understood the true character and nature of mature masculinity.

7 Get Male Support

Make no mistake about it: you need the support of men around you, men who respect what you're trying to do and who honour all your archetypal energies just as you do.

I recently led a weekend Lover archetype workshop for men only. Several men on this workshop had spent a long time steeped in the Tantric tradition where personal development work takes place mostly in mixed gender groups.

They were delighted and surprised about their new experience of working in a men-only group as opposed to a mixed gender group. The pleasure they found in being part of a male circle reminded me that men working together in a group with a common objective generate a special kind of energy which affirms them at the very core of their masculinity.

To put it another way, men understand men. Men get a lot from being with other men, consciously and unconsciously.

Of course we do! Why would we not? In my view, we are all more similar than different. And while most of us want a woman as a partner in relationship, there's no denying that men seem more at ease, more open, more authentic in a group of men than in a mixed gender group. There's a different energy when women are part of a group. I've heard the same from women, too.

The energy generated in a good men's group is something we desperately need in our society today. Men function better when they are not trying to do everything alone. They also need the support of men they can trust so they can allow themselves to be vulnerable. However, getting together with men in a men's group isn't about being an asshole and doing adolescent things. Nor is it about being a jerk or enjoying the company of other pumped-up men behaving like adolescent boys. (Though that can be fun for our inner children!)

A good men's group will give you a feeling for and an affirmation of true manhood, together with a sense of being with other men who understand you in a way that women simply can't. It's about having a place to share your deepest secrets with a group of men you trust. It's about sharing a space where you can be heard and witnessed by men who understand your experience as a man more deeply than you could ever imagine.

If you find a good men's group, you will find true buddies, men who may become friends for life with a very deep connection. This kind of connection is much deeper than going down the pub and watching sport together, though that can be fun too.

A group where men sit together and really hear each other's deepest truths is a group which engenders a deep sense of male bonding. I believe that if every man in the world found a men's group to support him in this way, the world would be a much better place. If you don't know the meaning of love for your brothers (and all men are your brothers), then find a men's group made up of open-minded men and discover it for yourself.

In such a group, you can learn to take the push of other men defending their boundaries, and you can learn to push back against them. You can learn to listen. You can work on your emotional wounds. And you can learn to clear the tensions that arise between men without violence, anger or fighting. You won't know how powerful this is until you experience it.

And once you've experienced it, you won't want to be without it. (If you can't find a men's group, you might even want to start one. Don't know how? Well, take the plunge! There is good information at www.mensgroupmanual.com and in the book *A Circle of Men: The Original Manual for Men's Support Groups* by Bill Kauth.)

The Boyhood Archetype Of The Warrior: The Hero And The Hero's Journey

The Hero archetype is probably the most advanced form of boy psychology, and normally the peak of adolescent masculine energy. Naturally, it's an immature archetype simply because it's an aspect of boyhood, and boyhood itself is an immature state of masculinity. So when a boy grows physically into a man but does not develop psychologically beyond the Hero, he cannot form a mature masculine identity. He remains a boy-man.

Adolescent boy-men are all around us in society. They are driven by impossible dreams, and they haven't yet recognized that these dreams are never going to come true. In fact, they haven't evolved from their adolescent mission into a true mission of their own, a mission which reflects their soul purpose. That transition is a step which every man must take before he can move into full male maturity and sovereignty.

So whether we look at a boy exploring the power of the Hero archetype or a man still locked in the grip of the Hero archetype, we see immaturity. Some men continue to behave heroically well into the later part of their lives when Elderhood and Sovereignty should be developing. This is a real case of inhibited development.

And yet, the Hero is an important archetype in men. Moore and Gillette believed that it was an essential part of our evolutionary adaptation. They thought every boy needed a Hero archetype to provide him with the energy to break free from his Mother at the end of his boyhood, as he faced the difficulties and challenges of life as a man. In this view of the archetypal structure of masculinity, the Hero provides the energy to boost a boy out of his dependence on and identification with mother into true male independence. Presumably it's also the energy which fuelled a boy through initiation rituals and rites of passage into manhood in societies where they existed.

To put it another way, the Hero archetype provides the energy which a boy needs so he can show his competence and prove himself strong enough to overcome – or at least survive – the forces which the world throws against him.

Moore and Gillette spoke of the Hero as an archetype that enabled the boy to establish "a beachhead" against the overwhelming power of the unconscious, much of which they believed is experienced as the feminine, specifically as mother, in men.

In this view, the Hero is an important archetype because it somehow embodies an ideal vision of what a boy could become as a man – if he is indeed able to overcome the forces of the world.

In archetypal legends the boy comes up against the forces of the world and defeats them, reigning supreme like Superman. In practice, this kind of spirit empowers a man to take action in the world to get what he wants. Although there may be hard lessons for him to learn before he grasps the reality and limitations of his abilities, strength and power, he will gain an understanding of what is possible for him and what is not.

The Hero archetype is generally not well-regarded in our age. Often those who dare to stand above the crowd or try to shine are dragged down by others of lesser ambition or ability. And in that lies one particular representation of the archetypal legend about the "Death Of A Hero, Birth of A Man" – a death which may be needed before the mature Warrior can take his rightful place.

The death of the Hero represents the death of boyhood and boy psychology. Hopefully this naturally allows for the birth of manhood and man psychology, a condition which provides the opportunity to experience humility and an understanding of one's true strength in the world. Humility combined with strength are qualities of the Sovereign. But if we continue to be possessed by the energy of the Hero into adult life we can never mature fully. We cannot take our place as a true Sovereign.

And should we fall under the shadow aspects of the Hero, our transition into mature masculinity will take even longer. In fact, it may never happen.

The Shadows Of The Hero Archetype

There are two shadows of the Hero: the inflated grandstanding bully, and the deflated coward.

A boy or a man under the influence of the grandstanding bully is all about impressing others. He wants everyone to know that he is superior, that he has the right to dominate. He has no sense of his true position in the world. When he's challenged about the way he behaves he may respond with verbal abuse, rage or even physical abuse. Does you see this in people in your world, or on the wider political scene in our times?

What underlies this shadow archetype is a deep sense of inferiority and insecurity. You can see this archetype playing out in so many ways: hotshot businessmen who refuse to be team players, bankers and financiers who buck the system for their own advantage (at the expense of the rest of us), immature men in the military who risk themselves and their men's lives to gain glory or establish a reputation, small men who somehow manage to inflate themselves into positions of power. And so on. You can smell the immature Hero a mile away.

If you've seen the movie *Top Gun*, you may recognize the immature Hero in the character played by Tom Cruise. He refuses to recognize the danger he's creating for himself and everyone around him. Only when he contributes to the death of his navigator and friend and later fails to win the competition for "Top Gun" does he begin to sense that he needs to move from adolescence to maturity.

The difference between Cruise's character and the more mature flyer called Iceman in the movie is the difference between Hero and mature Warrior.

The grandstanding bully is the inflated pole of the Hero's shadow. The mentality that goes along with this inflation is one of invulnerability, fighting the impossible fight, winning the unwinnable battle, dreaming and realizing the impossible dream.

No matter what the sense of invulnerability and the godlike pretensions of the boy-man with this immature energy may be, the truth is simple. Life will always have a cruel lesson for him: he cannot win against the world. Not in the end, anyway.

The Hero archetype has an overly close connection with mother or the feminine. In fact Moore and Gillette suggested that the Hero archetype was "locked in mortal combat" with both the inner feminine, the Anima, and the outer feminine, the Mother, in an attempt to escape and assert masculinity. Maybe so.

What's certain is that any boy or man under the power of the Hero archetype or its shadows does not fully understand he is a mortal being who is destined to meet the reality of the world head-on. Nor does he grasp that he will then inevitably suffer some kind of death, either spiritually, physically or emotionally. Some men reach their death-beds before they wake up to this unavoidable fact. Some don't wake up to it even then, and die fighting against death itself.

Heroic immaturity is rarely challenged in our society. Moore and Gillette said: "When we do not face our true limitations, we are inflated, and sooner or later our inflation will be called to account." Perhaps we now lack the Sovereigns who can call the Heroes to account.

What of the opposite shadow polarity, the deflated Coward?

Sadly, this is just as common in grown men as it is in adolescent boys. The Coward, as you might expect, will run away from the fight. In fact he probably runs away from anything and everything.

He may justify his refusal to fight by saying it's more manly to turn the other cheek or he may just live quietly with the humiliation of knowing he is a coward. Whatever, he usually allows himself to be bullied emotionally, intellectually and physically.

He caves in easily, he acquiesces to pressure from others, and his opinions are flexible. Of course he feels invaded and disrespected, and so, when he's had enough of being a doormat and can take no more, he may launch a verbal or even physical assault upon his opponent – which usually takes the opponent by surprise since this behaviour is so out of character.

Boys and men under the influence of this shadow lack the drive to achieve anything. But, as Moore and Gillette observed, "If we access the Hero energy appropriately, we will push ourselves up against our limitations. We will adventure to the frontiers of what we can be as boys, and from there, if we can make the transition, we will be prepared for our initiation into manhood."

In Summary

The Warrior is the part of us which goes out into the world and gets things done – on the orders of the King. He's an action taker, but a principled one, and he serves his King in support of a cause he believes in.

His internal discipline controls his rage. His anger is channelled appropriately for the situation he is in. That may be simply presenting the energy of action in the world, it may be showing assertiveness, or it may be establishing clear boundaries.

When necessary, the Warrior acts with clean anger to provide the energy of offensive or defensive action when that is needed to protect the things and people for whom he is responsible.

He may feel fear, but that will not prevent him from executing the King's Mission in the world, nor from bringing to an end those things which no longer serve the Kingdom.

With a clean, clear Warrior around, women, children and all the other citizens of the Kingdom feel much safer.

Chapter 3

The Magician Archetype

Look around you right now, and you'll see how archetypal magician energy influences every area of our lives.

Our amazing technology, every advance in our civilization, our capacity to dominate the world around us – all are the product of humanity's magician energy. Unfortunately this has both positive and negative aspects.

On the one hand we have the modern technology which serves us and can make our lives easier and more enjoyable. On the other hand there is a darker side which threatens our very existence. For example, think of the inhumanity of modern weapons of war and the insane amount of money spent on their development – money which, if put to constructive use, could probably solve all the world's problems.

So you can see immediately that there are some interesting paradoxes to the Magician. Is he good or bad? Moral or amoral? Helpful or unhelpful? The answer is a paradox: he can easily be both. But as we shall see, no matter what he's like in your life now, one of his earliest intentions was to protect you from harm as best he could.

Magician energy takes many forms, but the basis of them all is thinking rather than feeling. Your Magician archetype is the one which answers your questions. He knows how to find solutions to problems, how to create and master technology, and how to access and use your powers of creativity, reasoning, introspection, logic and intuition.

And the Magician is also the gatekeeper to altered states of consciousness, being a true master of ceremonies and rituals such as Rites of Passage. He controls our connection to a deeper level of consciousness, intuition, understanding and knowledge, a function of our brain which may go way back in history to a time before our thinking brain, the neocortex, evolved.

The Magician serves as our access point to all the mysterious connections between us and Planet Earth, and between us and all the other living creatures with which we share our planetary home. If you've ever asked the Universe for a sign, and received one, the Magician was your point of contact with the universal forces which responded to you.

No wonder, then, that when you access your Magician archetype, you're accessing an archetype that has been present in the human psyche throughout history.

According to Moore and Gillette, some anthropologists believe that long ago in our history the energies of the King, the Warrior, the Magician, and the Lover were not so closely linked as we see them today. In fact, so the theory goes, they were found together in only one man or woman in every society – the Chief.

The Chief manifested all of these archetypes in a whole-istic way – a well-integrated way. As time passed, the ancient archetypal energies separated and became more defined, to the point where the energies and roles of Warrior, Magician, Lover and King are identifiable and separate parts within ourselves and indeed also in our society.

So now we have Sovereigns in the form of Kings, leaders, and chieftains. These Sovereigns have their Warriors (in the form of armies) and their Lovers (sometimes internal, sometimes externalized as a Queen or as the feminine energy in society). They have their Magicians, too, also known as "experts", advisers, counsellors, wise men and wise women, sages, shamans, witch doctors, and wizards.

The same is true for each of us: we have a leader or Sovereign archetype in our internal system, a sub-personality if you like, whose rightful job is to be in control of our lives.

We have a Warrior archetype which goes out and gets things done. We have a Lover archetype within us which is responsible for connection with ourselves, with others, and with the world. And we have a Magician, our own internal wise man.

The Magician In His Fullness

Let's start by looking at some of the more notable qualities of the Magician archetype and seeing how these qualities manifest in our modern world.

The Holder Of Special Knowledge

The Magician archetype is traditionally the holder of secret or special knowledge which the other archetypes don't possess.

In ancient times Magicians held the knowledge of how to access altered states of mind and levels of consciousness. They knew the best time to plant the crops and they knew which gods should be propitiated, and when, with the appropriate ceremonies.

These Magicians, shamans, witch doctors, wizards and healers – call them what you will – also knew about medical herbs, healing potions and spells, and drugs that could access altered states. They knew how to bless and curse, and they understood the links between the unseen world of our ancestral spirits and the Earthly world we inhabit.

The Magician always was, and continues to be in some form or another, a source of information, guidance, support and instruction about this world and other-worldly matters. Nowadays you see him clearly in professional roles which require powers of analysis and divination: teacher, doctor, computer programmer, engineer, architect, psychotherapist, clairvoyant.

Because of his ability to think so clearly, to solve problems, and the way he can hold knowledge which is not common to all, the Magician has an enormous amount of power. He lives in you, regardless of your job, as an internal problem solver, creator, logician, thinker; he is your own high-powered internal super-computer.

One of the Magician's specialties is his understanding of how energy flows between and within individuals and societies. He's especially proficient in his understanding of the deep unconscious forces within us all. Developed and deployed with skill, the Magician's abilities to explore the unknown can be seen very clearly in his ability to access the unconscious mind. His wisdom and artistry always lies behind the skill of the best facilitators in counselling work, psychotherapy, emotional healing workshops, one to one archetypal coaching, and other forms of personal development work (page 179).

Master Of Technology

The Magician tends to be a master of technology. Throughout history, the creative force of the Magician archetype has propelled the development of all kinds of new knowledge and technology. He has brought us the extraordinary wonders of engineering, computing, science, music, literature and art we see around us today.

But the extraordinary thing is that the Magician is just as adept at building weapons of war as he is at building tools to encourage peace and harmony. He is just as good at planning destruction as building community. Here we see an important element of the Magician's way of working: he is not concerned with feelings so much as with results and outcomes. He needs to be given clear instructions by a wise and clear-sighted King to use his talents to their best effect.

He is the thinker *par excellence*, yet the consequences of his thinking often seem to be less important to him than the process of creation. He loves to create, to master technology, whether this is a weapon of war that will kill millions of people more efficiently than the last one he developed or an engineering innovation that will make drinking water available to millions of people through a radical new design of desalination plant.

In short, it would seem he hasn't got much emotional intelligence. Some people might call him lacking in conscience. And as we shall see, he can be exactly that and worse, for the sociopath and the psychopath are both shadows of the Magician archetype.

The Magician As Adviser To The King

Magicians help their Sovereigns, their Kings, make good decisions. They help Kings "think things through", using information obtained with their intuition, their acquired knowledge, their reasoning, and their creativity. But they are certainly not subservient to the King. In fact they have a special relationship with him.

More accurately, in the ideal relationship they are not subservient. Yet when a King becomes a tyrant, his Magician may be cowed or even turned to the Dark Side.

That's why there was a court joker or Jester in ancient European Courts. He was yet another expression of the Magician archetype. His role was specifically to deflate any King who began to get ideas above his station. The problem with Kingship is that often people don't dare to tell you when you're getting inflated or becoming too big for your own boots. So the Jester was tasked with the deflation of a pompous King who'd lost sight of his own limitations.

Generally, though, the Magician was a wise advisor and counsellor to the King. This support allowed the King to grow into a fuller and more mature masculine energy so that he became a better King. Often a group of magicians would form the King's Court – a group of King's counsellors or advisers. But because Magicians know their own importance, every King needs to treat them with respect, for only then can he be sure of gaining the help of his Magicians and his King's Court.

This is a very different dynamic to the one between the King and the Warrior. The Warrior takes orders and knows his place, but the Magician requires the King to treat him at least as an equal; he demands respect for the knowledge he holds and his ability to work with it.

If he doesn't get it, he may take his secret knowledge and use it for his own benefit – perhaps to the detriment of the King. Or he may switch allegiance and use it for the benefit of another King altogether. Allegiances and alliances with a Magician depend on more than the King's wishes; they also depend on the Magician's loyalty. And that depends on him having the King's ear.

Magicians who aren't regularly consulted tend to go off and mix potions in their laboratories, create formulae, find things to amuse themselves, and even wreak havoc, just for the curiosity of seeing what happens when they try out a new idea.

Rites Of Passage & Master of Ceremony

The creative power of our intellect allows us to develop new technology that seems to give us "dominance" over the world around us. This is one obvious outlet of magician energy, but there are many other ways in which the Magician's energy manifests in our world. Among them are some less obvious and less well-known processes which are very important in the human psyche.

One example is the creation of rites of passage and initiation rituals for men. Another way in which magician energy manifests is in the form of psychotherapy and other approaches to deep soul work such as Vision Quests and Shadow Work.

Access to the mysterious depths and complexity of such profound soul work is truly the province of the Magician. Contemporary Magicians who do deep work in psychotherapy understand that the forces and energies in our Shadow, in our unconscious, are so powerful that they must only be accessed to the right degree, at the right time. Without proper care, they can be too powerful for an individual man or woman to contain. In short, the Magician uses ceremony and ritual to establish control of energies which are beyond the understanding of the conscious mind.

The Magician: Doorkeeper To Our Unconscious

Every seeker after truth, every man or woman involved in the pursuit of self-development, is pursuing a quest for self-realization in some way. Certainly some of us are pursuing that path more intensely than others, but somewhere within each one of us the Magician archetype will be helping us work towards self-realization by offering the opportunity to look at our shadows.

While our ego, our sense of self, is essential for us to function in the real world, our archetypal shadows also control us and modify the expression of our ego. For us to grow as men into our full power these shadows need to be brought into the light and seen for what they really are – parts of ourselves which we suppressed into the unconscious a long time ago for some very good reason, and which now have the power to influence our behaviour.

However, your unconscious Shadows are only revealed to you at the rate at which you can handle them. Paradoxically, as soon as you achieve growth in your sense of self, more shadows pour out of your unconscious mind to challenge you. I think of it like this: once you've embarked on the path of personal development there's no turning back; it's a life-long commitment.

I was facilitating an Emotional Process Workshop some years ago on which a young man came up to me and asked me how old I was. I told him I was 54, and asked him how old he was. He told me he was 27, and went on to say something which seemed astonishing to me: "I can't wait to be your age because by then I'll have my life completely sorted out."

Not many young men have ever said this to me! I tried to explain this isn't how life works, at least not for anyone I've ever met. No matter how much sorting out we may have done there is always more to do. That's because the Magician, who is the gatekeeper to our unconscious, will only allow parts of our Shadow to emerge when he knows we are ready to hold the energy of the unconscious, and to hold it well enough that we will not be destroyed by it. My young friend wasn't having any of it, though: he was sure personal growth and development is a finite process. No doubt life will show him the truth in its own good time. The truth is our internal Magician is the real gatekeeper in our journey of personal development. He contains the enormous force of the unconscious and channels it at a rate we can cope with. And once he sees you are serious about your personal growth he will never stop offering you more challenges.

The Specialist

Doctors, lawyers, priests, businessmen, plumbers, therapists, computer programmers, designers, builders, electricians, in fact everyone who uses special or particular knowledge acquired by study and experience, all draw on the power of their Magician to convert their knowledge into a practical benefit for someone else.

On this level there is no difference between the technicians building the space shuttle, the computer programmers providing us with access to a vast array of technology on our smart phones and computers, the psychotherapist analyzing our complexes, and the Shaman with his rattles, herbs, and incantations. This specialist knowledge is one of the foundations on which the Magician's influence rests, for it is knowledge which can be used to achieve a particular outcome.

More Interested In Thinking Than Feeling

Magicians tend to detach, to take a higher or more distant perspective, at least emotionally, from what's going on in the world. Indeed, they often find solutions to problems without referring much to human feelings and emotions.

So while we can see technology all around us working for our benefit, we can also see how magician energy has led to the development of ever more complex technology used simply to kill and destroy each other all the way through our history to the present day.

Each war has driven the development of killing technology, so much so that we now have wars conducted remotely by drones piloted from bases deep inside countries far away from the killing fields. Previous generations of Magicians created gunpowder, cannons, machine guns, the concentration camps, nuclear weapons, and the neutron bomb, among other atrocious weaponry.

Advances in technology have also brought about progressively more ingenious ways to exploit natural resources: mountain top removal for coal, tar-sand extraction for oil, deforestation for timber and agriculture, and fracking for fuel, among many others. These technologies all carry their own consequential damage to our planet. They involve the production of evermore toxic waste without finding ways to dispose of it, oil spills in pristine wilderness areas, and other environmental catastrophes.

These are representative examples of how the energy of the Magician can manifest without conscience, awareness, or even much interest in the human consequences of what he produces. Mind you, Magicians can have a great time finding ways to clean up the messy consequences of their clever ideas.

Yet the deeper truth is that "solving the problem" seems to be enough for many Magicians. For example, the problem of coming up with cheap, reliable and strong packaging material for consumer goods was solved in the 1950s by the development of plastics. This has manifested in the production of around 300 million tonnes of plastic every single year at the time of writing, all of which is indestructible or practically indestructible.

Knowing this, you may wonder how the Magician can be so – well, let's call it uncaring – about the way his creations can cause such devastation and destruction. But to ask this question is to misunderstand his nature, for he is not at heart an emotional being. As an archetypal character, he may be more interested in achieving his objectives than in considering the possible consequences of doing so.

We see this in occupations where exclusive knowledge or a large element of privilege are essential. The financial traders who brought the banking system to its knees in the early years of this century could be said to embody magician energy. Without strong Sovereigns to guide them in the pursuit of benefits for the whole Kingdom, these magician-traders used their special access to "secret" knowledge for their own ends. The rest of us suffered the consequences.

It seems as though the line between employing unearned power and knowledge for the good of all and using it for personal benefit and profit is an easy one for the Magician to cross. The temptation to use magician energy for one's own ends, for example to boost the ego, or gain a reputation, or get what one wants (power, prestige, even sexual favours, perhaps) can be considerable.

The Safety Officer or Risk Manager

Fear resides very much within the Magician's area of influence. This is because fear arises in response to a threat to your safety or security, whether perceived or real. Often such fear signals the need for transformation or change; often it means that protective strategies are needed to keep you safe – and quickly! And both transformation and protection depend on the Magician's creativity and capacity to find solutions to problems.

So fear is a signal that something is about to change, either by choice or by force from outside you, and it can trigger your Magician, who is a master of transformation, into action.

If you had a difficult or challenging childhood, which would mean you felt a lot of fear, your Magician was most likely very active and creative in finding protective strategies for you from a very young age. These strategies could have included helping you to adopt particular ways of behaving in the world, the creation of a false persona to hide behind, or dissociation. In cases of very severe childhood wounding, the internal Magician uses Dissociative Identity Disorder as a protective mechanism.

Your Magician is especially likely to have produced such strategies to keep you safe if you faced physical, emotional or sexual abuse, or a violent, unpredictable or unstable environment as a child. This part of the Magician is known as the Risk Manager or Safety Officer.

However, the protective function of the Risk Manager is not limited to violent or abusive environments in childhood. A child's Risk Manager will grow in any environment where a child is subject to some kind of assault on his sense of self.

This might come from shaming or humiliation by family or peers, a lack of respect from relatives, or an unstable or unpredictable parent. It might come from being around family members who weaken a child's sense of self-esteem or self-respect, or who launch overt or covert attacks on his emotional or physical well-being. All of these threats, and many more, activate this part of the Magician archetype.

The Risk Manager's job is to come up with protective strategies, create defences against feeling shame, and find ways for a child to avoid being singled out as the neighbourhood victim or scapegoat. These strategies can be very creative, they can form very early on in life, and they can take many forms. Some of the more common ones include people pleasing, hiding yourself, avoiding being seen, never getting emotionally close to people, avoiding vulnerability, and lacking assertiveness.

The Risk Manager forms most of his strategies during childhood, so when he kicks in there can be a sense of regression in the air. For example, a man may once again "become" a little boy with no autonomy or Sovereign energy in the presence of a woman who seems to have some kind of power over him.

Unfortunately the boyhood Risk Manager will go on playing out the same defensive strategy for the rest of a man's life unless he seeks out someone who can help him with his emotional healing work. Since most boyhood strategies don't work too well in an adult relationship, achieving maturity as a man is important!

Sometimes these strategies appear as a pattern of offensive rather than defensive behaviour. Some Magicians clearly believe that "attack is the best form of defence." You know when you meet a Magician attached to this way of being – the verbal barbs come flying instantly, though you may not feel them until later.

I'm sure you can imagine that a strategy devised by a boy's Magician to help him feel safe and secure at the age of one, five, ten, fifteen, or even twenty is not necessarily in any way appropriate in a man aged forty, fifty or sixty. But unless the adult man does some relevant Emotional Process Work to heal his shadow, his ever-active Risk Manager tends to remain stuck developmentally in childhood. He's still doing the same things he came up with decades ago to keep the boy as safe as possible, even though he now lives in a man's body.

So the Risk Manager may prevent change by inculcating a kind of paralysis around risk. This can inhibit the normal processes of emotional development which should happen as a boy grows into a man. This paralysis, this lack of change, is based on running the old strategies which developed for very good reasons when the man was a little boy faced with a specific threat to his well-being.

This is why the initial stages of both one-to-one and group work using the archetypal model so often involve work with the Risk Manager. The aim is to get him to drop his defences, hopefully quickly and gracefully, so he can take on a new role which is much more appropriate to the man's life in the adult world.

That said, we must not underestimate the power and importance of the Risk Manager to a child who's now in, or has been in, a difficult environment. This part of the Magician can literally mean the difference between life and death for a child, whether that death would have been emotional, spiritual, or even physical.

So Risk Managers are one of the most vital manifestations of the Magician archetype. They can literally keep men and women alive and functioning. Unfortunately, as you can imagine, the price of the Risk Manager's risk management strategy can sometimes be very high for the adult man because it prevents him from achieving anything like his full potential.

Delicate and careful work with a man may be needed to reverse a lifelong strategy of fear-based behaviour now embodied in the energy of the Risk Manager. Fortunately, in Shadow Work and Emotional Process Work, where we work on the shadow unconscious, we have tools and techniques which can update the Risk Manager's job description without further threat to either the security of the adult man or the security of the little boy who still lives inside the adult man.

Accessing Deeper Consciousness

When we enter a deeper level of consciousness, we also access a deeper part of our mind. This might be the altered state of consciousness an artist uses to give birth to a masterpiece, a musician needs to give a spellbinding performance, or a student uses to memorize material before an examination. It might be the altered state produced by hypnosis in which self-transformation can take place. All these states of mind, and many more, are the province of the Magician.

* * * * *

The Magician and Other Archetypes

Your Magician works things out; he is a source of information and he provides solutions to problems. And just like the other archetypal figures he should not exist in isolation. In fact his role is to serve the King as his King's counselor. But in the absence of a strong King, a manipulative Magician may take control of the Kingdom and start running the show, perhaps issuing orders to the Warrior.

If your Magician influences your Warrior without your King's oversight or control, two things can happen. First, your Warrior can be empowered with strategic and tactical skills to take action in the service of the realm. Though not perfect, because the King is missing from the loop, this can sometimes be good enough. Second, your Warrior can be influenced to take action in the service of your Magician. Unfortunately that usually means doing something for the Magician's benefit, not the Kingdom's. This is a route to chaos. This is the way Kingdoms fall.

The way the system should work is this: your Sovereign has a problem. He asks your Magician to collect relevant information and advice. When he gets this, when he feels fully informed, your King can make a decision on what to do next. He then issues instructions to your Warrior to get out into the world and actually do something.

The kind of information you need might include finding out how to solve a particular problem in your life, how to support your children in their difficulties, how to overcome some limitation in your knowledge and understanding of the world, how to get a failing business back on track, how to finish the book which has been sitting partly written on the shelf for several years, how to talk to a business client about a contract, how to get a new project off the ground, and so on. Anything, in fact. Anything at all.

There are many possible ways to do this, but they all centre on you taking on the role of Sovereign in your world and asking a part of yourself – your Magician – to do what he does best: coming up with solutions to problems.

When he's given a clear request with obvious intention on your part, your Magician will discover some way to get the necessary information. You might find yourself doing some research on the internet, speaking to an expert, talking to other people, and so on. Later you have a moment of clarity, an "aha" moment, when you suddenly see what options are available to you and feel able to choose between them.

The point about this practice is that it makes your desires and intentions much more conscious. You are taking control of your mind by using these powerful archetypal metaphors. With that control, you can establish clarity about what is needed, and then decisions become easier and quicker – all because the different parts of your internal system know what they are doing, and why.

It's helpful to establish clear communication between King and Magician simply to keep good order in your Kingdom. A Magician left to his own devices without much Kingly contact tends to amuse himself by working for his own ends, and this can lead to chaos in the Kingdom.

Despite his mischief-making, there are many positive sides to the Magician. He just needs a good and wise King to control his actions and ensure he works for the benefit of all. Yet I believe a very real challenge we all face today in our world is the absence of powerful Sovereigns who can run their internal and external Kingdoms well and wisely, for the benefit of all, with compassion and integrity.

The Emotional Wound In the Magician Quarter

The emotional wound in the Magician consists of a belief, conscious or unconscious, that you're bad in some way.

This wound begins to grow in a child when people around him directly or indirectly convey the message "There is something wrong with you" or "You're different, shameful or bad" or even "You are evil" during childhood. Of course, these messages do not have to be spoken. As with any other archetype, they can be communicated by behaviour, body language and attitude as well as words.

As a result a child comes to believe an internal voice which whispers (or shouts) "You are bad," "You are useless," or one of the endless variations of "There is something wrong with you." This may evolve into a first person voice which is often very self-critical and harsh: "I am bad." "I am useless." "I can't do it."

As the child grows into a man, one or both of these internal voices may live on, constantly playing their harsh message of criticism and self-criticism. Unfortunately the adult man in whom they live may not recognize the harshness of the criticism and judgements. To him, it's all normal. It's always been normal. The internal dialogue here goes like this: "You are useless." "Yes I am."

Where there is emotional, physical or sexual abuse a child may internalize the energy of the abuser as though it were part of his own personality. At some level, the child may sense that energy within his own unconscious and believe it to be a part of him.

But why would a child absorb these beliefs about him or herself rather than simply rejecting them? The answer lies in the energy of shame. Some people call this toxic shame, an expression which sums up its impact very well: for shame really is poisonous to your soul and destructive of your well-being.

Shame is made up of both a bodily-based element and a cognitive element. It develops when a child is humiliated or judged negatively simply for being who he is or doing what he does. And it seems most of us carry shame at some level, because during childhood we've all somehow received the toxic message that we're bad, to a greater or lesser degree.

Shame can hide in the body for decades, unsuspected, before it finally manifests, perhaps well into our adult lives, as a peculiar feeling of discomfort throughout the body. Often people do not know what this feeling is and mistake it for embarrassment, fear or guilt.

The cognitive element of shame is made up of the negative beliefs we hold about ourselves. In its simplest form the shaming message for a child in the Magician quarter is "You're a bad boy." Generally the message of badness is conveyed in more subtle or specific ways. Take religion, for example.

Time and again in my work I come across the shame carried by those born into "devout" Christian families. Christianity is a religion founded on the concept of original sin, so you're damned from the moment you're born, carrying this original sin. Men who were educated in certain Catholic schools, especially those administered by the Christian Brothers, tell me they were constantly reminded how bad they were, sometimes in the most brutal ways. The boys were told they were evil and treated accordingly, mostly by teachers trying to beat the badness out of them.

Such religious-based messages and sadistic behaviour carry a fundamental shaming based on the assumption of one's essential worthlessness and badness. These cultural messages unequivocally tell you that you're bad from the inside out.

Shaming comes in many other forms, though. In my work I meet a lot of men and women who were shamed for their sexuality and sexual urges both before and after puberty. One client who I guided through his healing had been brought up in a puritanical religious family. When he was a young boy, every time his grandmother noticed him holding or playing with his penis, she told him he would go to hell. Being a bright child, he concluded that he really must be bad and that there must indeed be something fundamentally wrong with him. After all, in his child-like Magician's mind, hell was where bad people were sent.

There are many more subtle ways in which children pick up a message of shame and badness about themselves. If a child is punished for simply being who he is, or "disciplined" in a way that conveys the clear message of "You're bad" or "We don't like you" or "We don't like you when you behave in a certain way", then a sense of inherent badness or shame can develop.

I also see this a lot in adults who were physically, emotionally, or sexually abused as children. The reasoning in a child's mind is "This is happening to me because I am bad" or "This wouldn't have happened to me unless I deserved it." This logic reflects a child's inability to see that his parents or carers are really responsible for what is happening to him, and that the fault does not lie with him.

When a child is given to understand that he's bad, he's likely to react by trying to change the way he behaves so that he regains his parents' love. He might do this by making a mental adjustment to the way he sees the world. This can mean unconsciously detaching or slightly dissociating from himself; or, as I see it, stepping out of his soul so he can observe himself.

The Magician logic behind this reaction is easy to understand. If you can catch yourself before you do something "bad", and then stop yourself doing it, you'll be safe from fear, shame, punishment, disconnection, humiliation or something else equally painful.

However, the problem is that although stepping out of yourself in this way can be an effective strategy for staying safe, it often leads to a child (or an adult) being told he is cool or detached. The boy is then being shamed for the very strategy that was supposed to keep him safe from shame.

He may then take another step out of himself, his thinking being that if he can observe his own behaviour from a higher or more distant vantage point, he'll be able to pre-empt the thoughts which lead to his behaviour being labelled as bad, and so avoid the fear or shame that would otherwise come his way.

Of course he's then even more detached and the reaction he gets to that is being told he's manipulative, detached and unfeeling, which in some sense he is, of course.

Eventually, if this process continues, he may have stepped out of himself so much that somewhere along the way he lost connection with his feelings and his sense of self. Such parenting is a good way to grow a sociopath, or at least to raise a child who spends the rest of his life trying to regulate others' feelings in an attempt to stay safe by creating an element of predictability in his world. Unfortunately this supposed safety comes at the expense of his own feelings and his connection to other people.

Even so, the ability to dissociate in this way is a great asset to a child who grows up in an environment which reeks of danger and fear. When there is the constant threat of physical violence or emotional abuse, being on guard and staying watchful are strategies which may pre-empt trouble and help a child avoid unpleasant experiences.

But the cost is high: the child lives in a constant state of emotional arousal – which we might call anxiety or fear – because he is hyper-vigilant 24/7 about the threat of what might or might not happen next. This is a logical defence in an environment which has the potential to hugely shame or damage the child, but the defence carries its own high price too.

That price is living in a state of fear, maybe spending a lot of time dissociated, and perhaps developing an internalized self-hatred and sense of shame about your very existence. Such a profile is definitely not going to help you fully connect with other people or develop healthy emotional connections.

In a world which puts so much value on being seen as "good", and even demonizes those seen as "bad", the almost inevitable result for any child who believes he or she is essentially bad is a deep – but possibly unfelt – sense of shame about their existence. A strange thing about this shame is that it's not easy to find in the body in the way that other emotions are. It hides. It's hard to pin down. And no wonder, because it's a state of being rather than a feeling.

Generally if you ask somebody where their anger is located, they can show you by putting a hand on a particular part of their body. But ask somebody where their shame resides and most likely they won't be able to do that. This is because shame is somehow imprinted in every cell of the body. It's all over, everywhere. It's hard to find until it comes out of hiding and hits you unexpectedly. Then you know about it.

Shame can be narrow, and shame can be broad. For example, you might carry shame around your sexuality, or you might carry a more widespread feeling of shame about your very existence somehow being bad or wrong. Whatever form it takes, this wound requires delicate and skilful handling by anyone with a therapeutic intention. Nowhere is that more true than in the arena of sexual or physical abuse.

For a therapist, dealing with magician energy can be challenging, particularly when a man's Magician has evolved into a very skilled and clever character in response to the original emotional wounding. Unless he has the skills to handle it, a therapist can be led a merry dance by a cunning Magician whose every action is designed to prevent the therapist from seeing either the emotional wound or the real person who hides behind the defences erected by their Magician.

Often someone with a deep wound in the Magician quarter will say "I can't feel anything" or "I don't know how to feel." But sometimes it's not so much that they can't feel, more that they're choosing not to feel, or at least choosing not to know what they're feeling. This can be another Magician defence against feeling (or even acknowledging) the intense level of fear with which they once lived.

Healing work in this quarter often starts by getting the Risk Manager to consider giving up his lifelong pattern of protective strategies. The problem is that the Risk Manager prefers to take no chances. He does what he does because it was useful once upon a day. And because he works out of sight, mostly in an unconscious way, he doesn't get much exposure to new ways of doing things. In any case he's probably the one running the Kingdom because there isn't a strong Sovereign on hand to change the way things are done in the realm.

In our Emotional Process Workshops we sensitively interview and honour the part of a man's Magician which has acted as his Risk Manager since childhood. We are experienced in working with this part of the psyche, and we find that many Risk Managers are delighted to take on an updated job description and are very happy to support change when they understand the advantages it can bring to their "host".

Just like all the other shadow archetypal energies, Magician energy can inflate or deflate in response to emotional wounding. These two polarities are the manipulator or predator in the inflated pole, and the innocent or confused one in the deflated pole of shadow.

The Inflated Shadow Magician: The Predator

The inflated shadow energy of the Magician produces the manipulator or predator. This is a manifestation of the Magician archetype in which a man's Magician uses his skill cunningly and ruthlessly, even perhaps without conscience, to obtain and express influence and power in the world.

There is a detachment from emotional connection here which may lead to cynicism, victimization, cruelty and predation. In its most extreme form this complex manifests as the psychopath, an individual who is totally detached from his own humanity.

The origins of this shadow lie in the childhood emotional wounding which caused the Magician to detach from feeling and connection with other people and the world around him. Yet underpinning all of this cynicism, manipulation and detachment lies deep and profound fear.

Sure, fear can protect us and alert us to danger, but it can also make us detached, disconnected and withholding. Fear may cause us to use our knowledge as a weapon with which we can disempower others and at the same time bolster our status, wealth or power. Such black magic is indeed the currency of the inflated Shadow Magician.

The Deflated Magician

On the other hand, the deflated Magician, the passive pole of the Shadow Magician, manifests as the fool, the simple one, or the confused one who does not know. What does he not know?

Anything, really. This shadow is powerlessness. It's an avoidance of taking responsibility, an avoidance of being the Magician in charge of something important.

This passive shadow is characterized by a lack of energy, effort, power, or even real presence in the world. All this shadow wants is enough power to interfere with those who are making forward movement in the world.

This shadow of the Magician always appears to be innocent and unknowing. But this innocence hides a desolation and deep wounding of the individual, a wounding so deep that he is in some sense "lifeless". He cannot take responsibility for his presence in the world. He may adopt an air of detachment, of aloof superiority, even an impressive knowingness, but his cynicism, his deflating remarks, and his hostility towards other people (always disguised as humour) show through anyway. This is an act designed to create a wall so strong that it keeps others separate, apart, away.

You may find it hard to confront a man (or woman) with this shadow. He lacks Warrior energy, he lacks the power to cut through to the truth. His Magician is in control. His defence is often a subtle kind of manipulation, an endless debate fuelled by circular thinking which never reaches a conclusion – and even if it does, that conclusion will most likely be reversed next time you speak.

A shadow Magician keeps answers and clarity out of your grasp and can hypnotize you with an energy of entrancement which leads you to engage with him at his level. That's a trap, for you will surely enter an endless maze of questions, an endless conversation, which goes nowhere and achieves nothing.

When challenged, shadow Magicians are adept at discharging their own shame on to you while they slip away, maintaining their innocence, and you are left feeling ashamed for having seen them in such a negative light or somehow thinking the whole problem is your fault. And yet at the same time your own Magician will sense you've been manipulated and outwitted, and you'll be left questioning where the truth lies.

How To Be A Balanced, Fully Present Magician

1 Study and Learn New Things

Since this is the realm of thinking, reasoning, and creativity, studying almost anything will take you deeper into the energy of the Magician. Of course you'd be wise to choose something you're interested in, to make the whole journey more enjoyable!

That might be learning the intricacies of a complex card game like bridge. It might be learning about a pastime that appeals to you: painting, pottery, winemaking, brewing, dancing, woodworking, fishing, hunting, or cookery, for example. It might be taking a personal development course or training in some new area of expertise such as computer programming, Greek mythology, or psychotherapy. It might involve a course of study or a change of job.

Whatever it is, it needs to be something you are drawn to, something which already appeals to the Magician within you, so that you have plenty of enthusiasm and passion to drive you forward in your pursuit of knowledge.

Magicians are traditionally long-lived beings in myth and legend. You might want to emulate that quality by becoming a lifelong learner and maintaining an active interest in gaining new knowledge for as long as you possibly can.

2 Enhance Your Creativity

You may or may not have noticed that mature men – which is to say emotionally mature elders, not just older men – seem to have a certain solid quality about them, a more substantial *presence*.

One reason for this is that they've evolved emotionally and spiritually. Often they've escaped the grip of consumerism, moving beyond it to a place of greater emotional maturity where the transient attraction of an endless supply of consumer goods is replaced by a deep appreciation of their real needs. In other words, they know themselves and they know what really matters to them.

They understand that satisfaction and happiness come from the inside, not the outside. They know that wanting something because it makes you feel better, look better, or because it makes up for some inherent deficiency in your sense of self is an immature way of being in the world.

Consumerism feeds into an inherent desire in the human species to accumulate wealth and goods as protection against hard times. However, a man with a mature Magician knows that any social opportunity (such as consumerism) which feeds into one of our intrinsic genetic "programs" (such as accumulating food or goods as a protection against hard times) is a distraction from the path towards mature masculinity and a diversion from personal growth.

To be powerful enough to resist the draw of consumerism, which in this case means giving up the transient "reward" of buying things you most likely don't *really* need, requires a strong Magician who has worked out a better way of being in the world.

One way to get the sense of fulfilment which buying and owning things can give you, but in a more healthy and permanent way, is to put your mental and physical energy into creating something of value. And so you might want to learn the art of woodcarving, learn how to strip down and rebuild steam engines, restore vintage cars, or write a novel.

There are countless ways to express your creativity: take up gardening, learn the art of metal forging, try your hand at painting, discover how to create great experiences for your family and friends, follow a spiritual path through life... the possibilities are indeed endless.

The key here is to engage with life in an active way rather than slumping passively in front of your computer, smart phone or TV every evening. Such an attitude dulls your Magician's edge and convinces him that there's no point in serving you because the demands placed on him are so far beneath his capacity.

3 Explore Your Soul

The domain of your Magician is your unconscious, the realm of your soul. If you're new to the exploration of soul and you wish to know more, start by finding the path that's right for you. This might be a particular path of personal growth and development such as psychotherapy, Shadow Work, or Emotional Process Work. You might want to go on a Vision Quest, or spend time in nature in some other way. Whichever path you choose, the more you dive deeply into your soul, the more your Magician energy will strengthen and develop.

4 Get Initiated into Manhood

Deep in the very fibre of his being every man wants – and needs – to truly understand what it means to be a man. And in fact every man needs – and wants, whether consciously or not – to be initiated into manhood by other men.

This is what men have always needed and still need to this day: to go through an initiation, a Rite of Passage which sets each of us on the road from boyhood or adolescence to mature masculinity. Without this transition a man may never come to naturally embody the energy of the mature masculine; he may remain adolescent in his thinking and attitude until he dies, incomplete and unformed as a man.

There are a few organizations offering modern-day Rites of Passage and rituals which serve as a contemporary form of traditional male initiation processes: the ManKind Project (mankindproject.org) and Illuman (illuman.org) are two examples. But are their offerings true initiation rituals? No, they are not. The nature and content of traditional masculine initiation rituals in which boys and men faced a real possibility of dying cannot be replicated in modern society.

Even so, these modern Rites of Passage have enough authenticity about them to speak to a deep part of your masculine soul. And initiation doesn't have to take place at a certain time of life: you can be initiated into manhood at any age. Whenever the process happens, it will still activate the part of you which has been waiting for years to come alive. It's important, though, to know that these modern rituals and ceremonies only work for men who are psychologically ready to make the transition from adolescence to mature manhood. Does that include you?

5 Join A Group of Initiated Men

Perhaps it is only in a group of men prepared to listen fully and hold space for you while you reveal your soul's longings and your deepest emotional wounds that you will feel truly safe and "at home".

You might want to start such a men's group or you might want to join one that already exists, such as those available to men who have undertaken the Initiation Adventure offered by the ManKind Project.

6 Create Sacred Space in Your Life

If you want to nurture the archetypal energy in your life, you will need a place where you can carry out your own rituals of connection with the various parts of your inner world. For example, you might go into your garden every morning for a few minutes to connect with each of your archetypal energies and ask them what they require of you as their Sovereign, or to give them instructions as you see fit.

Or you might have a room in your house where you can go to meditate or talk to each of your archetypes. You might spend time on a Vision Quest to discover what you need to know about the course of your future life. Above all, you might want to be a part of a men's group.

Every two weeks I meet with a group of men in the woods around a fire, come rain or shine, where we share our experiences of life, the world and masculinity. We support each other in our shared journey to healthier masculinity and together we experience the strength of brotherhood. My Magician loves it – and so does my Lover, my Warrior, and my Sovereign.

So set apart some area of your life, some experience you can call your own, something you can adopt as your own sacred ritual. You might have an altar or area representing each of the archetypes in a room in your house. You might have a place in nature where you can go to have these internal dialogues. Ask your Magician what is needed and see what he says.

Do this not only for the sake of your Magician but also for the rest of your internal Kingdom.

The Boyhood Archetype Of The Magician: The Precocious Child

The boyhood archetype that precedes the mature Magician is the Precocious Child. According to the dictionary, when applied to a child, the word precocious means "having developed certain abilities or inclinations at an earlier age than is usual or expected". And so it is, for although this archetype prefigures the mature Magician, some of its foremost qualities are the need to learn, the need to know how things work, and the need to understand why things are the way they are.

The stronger this archetype in a boy, the higher his performance in school, the earlier he learns to read, the better able he is to learn to play musical instruments, to excel at sports, and so on.

You see, this is the archetype which lies behind our urge to explore life. It drives our curiosity, delights in the astounding discoveries just waiting for us, and knows that everything is a mystery simply waiting to be explored and understood!

The motivation and energy of the precocious child is all about *understanding* as much as possible. And for some people, the way it lives on into adulthood becomes very important: it forms the basis of connecting with other people through the sharing of knowledge and understanding. For men in particular, this is an important way of connecting: to stand together on the ground of mutual interests and common understanding.

Moore and Gillette observed that the Precocious Child in a man "keeps his sense of wonder and curiosity alive, stimulates his intellect, and moves him in the direction of the mature Magician". You see, there is nothing wrong with the idea of the Precocious Child in itself. Difficulties arise when a child puts this innocent, wondrous boyhood archetype into shadow.

The Shadows of The Precocious Child

Like all archetypes, the Precocious Child has his own shadows.

The Inflated Trickster

This archetype trips us up, trips others up, misleads us, fools us, and ultimately betrays us. It's a manipulative energy which precedes and prefigures the manipulative and controlling energy of the inflated shadow Magician in adulthood.

Trickster plays out in a boy who wants everybody to know how clever he is. He is a "show off", he knows all the answers, he may be scathing of others, and he is always eager to prove how knowledgeable and intelligent he is.

A man still possessed by this immature shadow form of the Precocious Child archetype may alienate everybody else with his cocky attitude and his superior bearing. He knows all the answers; in fact he needs to know all the answers to feel good, and if he doesn't, well, there's no harm in making them up to fit. He tries to dominate others in discussion. He can be dismissive and disrespectful of those who don't know the answers or have a different opinion to him.

This is a juvenile energy which is about deceiving others, and perhaps deceiving oneself as well. What's that deceit about? About the depth of the knowledge you possess and your importance. This sounds painful, and it is, yet there is a function here: the Trickster can make trouble simply for the sake of exposing the fraudulent and deluded nature of those who live in their inflated egos. In a way he's determined to expose the shadow side of everything which looks too good to be true. And true to form, the Trickster is quite capable of doing this to you as well as to others.

We've all had experiences such as leaving only just enough time to make the journey from home to friends, office or appointment – and suddenly finding the car keys are missing. Or finding the ink on the printer runs out half way through an important document, no matter how well-prepared we thought we were. This is how Trickster shows himself.

Trickster is certainly a powerful archetype, and on the face of it an unhelpful one. Anybody in the grip of the Trickster tends to curse him every time he plays his tricks. But he is good at puncturing hubris and bringing us down-to-earth by showing us reality, clear and simple.

The problem with Trickster energy is that it can become destructive of you and everyone around you. The Trickster doesn't want any responsibilities. In fact he doesn't really want anything, except perhaps to create mischief. And even if there is a function to this – puncturing our hubris and grandiosity – it can be very unhelpful, upsetting and tedious.

The Trickster arises because we've been emotionally abused by our parents or siblings. We've been denigrated, attacked, told or shown, somehow, that we count for nothing, and as a result we've naturally forgotten our very special, even divine, nature, which is every child's gift to the world. So where there is an absence of appreciation accompanied by a need to hide who we really are, we come under the influence of the Trickster. His aim is to bring everybody down to the same level. And so we start to attack others who seem to be special; that way, we can deflate them to our own level. (Or, more accurately, the level to which we have been brought by others telling us untruths about who we are.)

Certainly the Trickster admires no-one. To admire someone is to have a hero. But Trickster wants to destroy the heroes who stand out, not celebrate them. The point is this: we can only admire others if we have a strong sense of our own worth.

So the way to disempower this polarity of the shadow Precocious Child is to get in touch with our own magnificence, our own special uniqueness, our own beauty, and our own creativity. Trickster needs a blessing to see his own beauty!

Formed as he was out of the devastation inflicted by our parents or siblings, who taught us that we were worth nothing, the qualities that defeat the Trickster are appreciation, love and acceptance.

The Deflated Unknowing One

The opposite, deflated, pole of the Precocious Child is the naïve, deflated "Unknowing One". This is the child who seems slow, unresponsive, or dull. He can't learn what other children learn as quickly or as easily as they can. He misses the point of jokes and is often physically uncoordinated. He is always the last one to learn about anything important and is usually a figure of fun for the neighbourhood boys. But this appearance may disguise real cleverness.

What seems to be happening here is that the boy has a hidden special quality, even a grandiosity, perhaps, that he knows is too important to be shown to the world. To reveal it would make him vulnerable. Acting dumb becomes a way to stay safe, or at least a way not to expose his magnificence, even though the pain of being the scapegoat in his family or the victim of other boys' taunts may be hard to bear.

As with all archetypes, the two polarities of inflation and deflation here, the Trickster and the Unknowing One, offer two places to hide. A boy may switch between them but one way or another the deeply wounded Precocious Child always seeks to hide his special qualities.

The problem is that he's never been encouraged to show how clever he truly is by his parents who, instead, have probably spent a great deal of time abusing and shaming him and denying his abilities rather than celebrating and honouring him.

In Summary

The Magician is the powerhouse of our intellect, the part of us which works out possibilities, the agent of safety in our lives, and a creative archetype which seeks ways to get what we want.

He can provide a way to connect with others through mutual understanding or shared interests. But at the same time he may lack emotional awareness, being more interested in achieving his objective than considering the possible consequences of what he is doing. Such matters are, after all, more the responsibility of his Sovereign. What he does feel is fear; accepting fear as a symbol of transformation and the need for things to change, he can create strategies and options from which the King can choose the best way forward.

Fear comes from the same roots as our feelings of excitement, so an intellectual reframe of fear, which lets us experience it instead as the excitement associated with new possibilities, can provide the Risk Manager, who lives in the Magician quarter, with enough motivation to change his old patterns of protection and explore new ways of being in the world.

Chapter 4

The Lover Archetype

Mention the Lover archetype, and thoughts of love and sex may come to mind. And it's true: love and sex are important aspects of Lover energy, but what really lies at the heart of the Lover archetype is a desire for connection. That is, connection with others, connection with ourselves, and connection with the planet on which we live.

The Lover archetype also serves as the container for our great primal hungers around sensuality, food, and emotional well-being. In fact the Lover is the most primal archetype for it springs into life the moment we are born.

Under the influence of the Lover we do our best to bond with our mothers after birth to ensure our protection and survival. And then we spend the rest of our lives trying to connect with other people in one way or another. If we cannot connect for any reason, we suffer; to be alone is not the natural destiny of the human animal.

Because it's so primal the Lover archetype continues to play a profoundly significant role in each of our lives for as long as we may live.

The Lover In His Fullness

The Lover in his fullness is all about feeling, not thinking. Some people think of the inner child as living here, but this is not completely accurate. Every archetype has childlike parts as well as older parts. Indeed, every archetype contains thoughts, feelings and behaviours all the way from birth to adulthood.

But it is true that the Lover archetype is the domain of the "free child", a state of innocence unencumbered by the demands of life. Many qualities associated with this idealized experience of childhood reside here, particularly innocence, pure love, unfettered attachment, idealization, spontaneity, sadness and tears.

The main qualities of this archetype in its fullness, its most mature form, are described below.

Sensuality

Because the Lover archetype is so much about sensuality and sensory experience in the body, much of the Lover's archetypal energy is inevitably associated with the body.

Our body is the first means of communication we have with our parents: immediately after birth our skin to skin connection with mother affirms our existence. Many other sensuous pleasures make up our world: feeling warm and safe, being held, experiencing a loving touch, and the pleasure of mother's milk.

And to reinforce the connections we are gradually forming, we have an instinct to gaze into the eyes of our carers so we connect and bond with each other. (Looking deeply into the eyes of our sexual partners in adulthood can reconnect us with the loving vulnerability of our inner child, who desires to connect with another more than anything else.)

Connection and Contact

When you hold a young baby who is being well cared for and whose needs are being met you can sense the innocent energy of the Lover archetype in its purest form. And when you see the steady, trusting look of a baby as he connects with his carers through mutual eye gazing, you see lover energy at work in one of its most profound ways.

All these needs for connection and contact remain with us as we move through life and grow and develop, though they become more expansive and take different forms.

Our desire for sexual connection with another human being is a fundamental element of the Lover archetype, but it may not be as important as simple non-sexual social and physical contact with other humans. Harlow's experiments with monkeys in the 1950s showed how baby monkeys deprived of physical contact with their mothers failed to thrive even though they had all the food and water they needed.

Failure to thrive in the absence of maternal contact is a human condition, too. But failure to thrive is not only about what happens in infancy. As primates, we are social animals. We are designed to be in a group, and to be a part of the social dynamics of that group. Maybe that's what helps to keep us sane, helps to preserve our humanity. Prisoners put into solitary confinement for extended periods soon develop mental and emotional problems, if not outright madness.

Sensitivity

The Lover holds our sense of connection with other people as well as our sense of connection with ourselves and with the Natural World.

You know that special feeling you get when you pause to really see and appreciate a beautiful sunrise or sunset, or when you're standing in the middle of an ancient forest hearing the sounds of the birds and sensing the energy of an unspoiled place which has existed for thousands of years? Both are a product of your archetypal Lover's capacity for feeling.

So both sensuality (feeling something which stimulates or delights the senses) and sensitivity (the quality of being sensitive to what's around you) are qualities of the Lover archetype. Sensitivity can take the form of heightened awareness of all things, both internal and external. Sensitivity is not an intellectual experience; it's more a felt experience, an emotional experience. When you're in your Lover, you want to touch and to be touched, both physically and emotionally.

Lack of Boundaries

The earliest expression of the Lover archetype is the bonding of mother and baby, both before and after birth. This union appears to be a state of existence for the baby in which he and mother are experienced as one and the same; there's no sense of separation between them in the baby's consciousness. Child psychologists tell us that a baby only becomes aware of itself as a separate being after a few months of life.

We may feel that experience of unity again during adulthood, at least to some degree, during the moment of orgasm when there seems to be a loss of self, a loss of the boundaries between lovers.

Insights such as these might make you think that the ultimate desire of the Lover archetype is to experience unification with everything around us – and you could well be right.

Some people, especially sensitive, spiritually inclined men and women with strong Lover energy, report an experience of touching a universal consciousness where they feel a sense of connection to the world beyond the boundaries of their own being. You may know of this experience yourself. So perhaps the mind really does have no boundaries. Mystics, clairvoyants, spiritual gurus, and "sensitive" people have believed this throughout history, and in many societies mystics have been accorded a special place because of their apparent ability to connect with a higher power.

As you see, our sense of spirituality lies firmly in the preserve of the Lover. Unfortunately, in my experience, many people use their spiritual practice as a defence against looking at what may be in shadow in all the archetypal quarters. The words "I've evolved beyond all that" or something similar have been offered to me on more than a few occasions by people unwilling to look into their shadow!

Most of us experience the Lover archetype in more subtle ways than a sense of universality. We experience it in our appreciation of the world around us, our appreciation of beauty, and in our joy and delight in sensory experiences of all kinds – the touch of a lover during sexual connection, the taste of exquisite food, the sound of soulful music, the sight of a powerful piece of art.

Those who live more in a Magician space can find it challenging to understand the feeling world of the Lover. The Magician relies on logic, on intellect, on reasoning; the Lover relies on sensation, insight, and feeling, and has no need to explain what is known and unknown. To feel is enough.

Grief

The Lover has a close relationship with the Sovereign because access to the joy of the Sovereign is only possible when the shadow grief of the Lover has been mostly brought into consciousness. But where does that grief come from and what is its purpose?

Quite simply this: we are genetically "programmed" to experience grief when we lose something of value or when an emotional connection is broken. And the hard truth is that you will inevitably lose everything you love, everything to which you are connected, sooner or later. These are the losses which will cause you grief.

So sensitive are we, in the Lover archetype, that we also feel grief around the loss of things we should have had but which we never experienced. That might include, for example, good parenting, a childhood full of innocence and wonder, the caring love of our parents, or the support and attention of wise elders.

So all love and all connections can bring us both joy and grief: joy when we have them and grief when we lose them. We even feel grief when we do not get the love and connections which we have a right to expect simply because we're alive. Our grief then is about the absence of what should have been ours yet never was.

For some reason, in our society we characterize grief as being "painful". Yet this pain is really the pain of grief which is *not* expressed – perhaps grief in response to the loss of a loved one, or the threat of the loss of a loved one, or a breaking of connection with a loved one, or the loss of objects and experiences which were valuable to us in some way. We can also feel a sense of loss and grief when we wanted something passionately but never had it.

When grief is finally expressed, when tears flow, the pain of loss diminishes and ease and grace take its place. When enough tears have flowed, joy appears and the gateway to the Sovereign begins to open naturally. After all, if you shut yourself off from your grief how can you expect to experience your joy?

Moving Beyond Love

Let's return for a moment to the concept of the Lover as an archetypal energy which goes well beyond love.

Somebody who lives mostly from the archetype of their Lover is not interested in boundaries, particularly socially created boundaries. The Lover, with his desire to merge and his disdain for boundaries, takes up a natural position against such things. And this manifests in his lifestyle: often messy, unconventional, even chaotic!

You can see, perhaps, how the energy of the Lover is so different to the Warrior's desire for boundaries and discipline, to the Magician's desire for logic and order, and to the King's desire for clarity, purpose and mission.

Yet the Lover archetype is essential to our humanity. He or she may flow around our psyche and energize our bodies, swirling out into the world around us in everything we do. We feel our sexual urges when we would rather not. We experience our desire for sensual satisfaction and immediate gratification more often than we would like. When unbounded these desires lead us to over-indulge in food, drink, drugs, sex, pornography, and our own particular addictions, about which we will talk more in a little while.

Many men project the energy of their Lover archetype out onto the feminine in general and a specific woman in particular. Others suppress and deny it. But by projecting, denying, or pushing this part of ourselves into shadow we create an energetic tension within our being which then needs to be soothed with sensuous and sensual pleasures. For the sake of our emotional wholeness each of us needs to fully embrace the Lover archetype within and allow the expression of its sensitive and sensual nature in the way that suits it best.

Embracing Love

In our society men are traditionally more focused on the energy of the Warrior and women more on the energy of the Lover. Yet there is a false dichotomy here, because we all carry Lover energy within us; it springs from the roots of connectedness between baby and mother or baby and father, and it helps us develop a wider social network as we grow older.

As we grow we become more emotionally sophisticated, and Lover energy drives us to experience different forms of love: brotherly love, sexual love, romantic love, love for ourselves, love for the planet on which we live.

Such is the male constriction on feelings in general and love in particular that many men will never experience the profound bond of brotherly love. This sense of non-sexual connectedness with another man resides in the Lover quarter and comes from an open-hearted place of mutual respect, connection, understanding and, yes, love.

Appreciation

Any artistic creation which evokes a sensual response draws upon the energy of the Lover. This includes our appreciation of literature, poetry, sculpture, dance, design, aesthetics, masculine and feminine beauty, as well as much else.

The Lover is the part of us which appreciates the sensuous touch of a massage therapist, the pleasure of holding a lover's hand, and our sense of peace and joy as we sit in silent connection with a friend watching the sunset together.

We feel the Lover's energy in the grace of time spent with children in those peaceful moments before they fall asleep. We feel it when we stop to smell the flowers as we walk through a beautiful garden. We feel it when we appreciate the sensuous delights of a finely crafted dinner or a fine wine. This is the energy that allows us to appreciate art and beauty, whether that be the soft touch of a finely sculpted piece of wood or the appreciation of a magnificent Renaissance panting.

When we're in our Lover archetype and its energy is in balance, the whole world looks optimistic, joyous, gracious, and perfect in every way.

You get the idea, I'm sure: the Lover loves connection and sensual experience of any kind.

Spirit v Soul

The Lover is a spiritual being rather than a soulful being. The Lover looks for unity with the world beyond himself, using the unconscious mind as a gateway to connect with something bigger – universal intelligence or cosmic consciousness, if you like.

This contrasts with the soulful energy of the Magician, which we can picture as going downwards and inwards to access the astounding force of the unconscious – the soul – for its own purposes.

The Lover, Love and Sex

As we know, sex is a powerful and important part of the Lover archetype, particularly for men. There's no getting away from the fact that while women may be driven by romance, sensuality and the very idea of love, men are very much driven by the act of love, the physical expression of the sexual energy within us.

As for love, well, we men project much of our capacity for love onto the feminine and allow women to carry it for us. However all of us men have a massive capacity for love – if we allow ourselves to feel it.

Men's love tends to be a very nurturing and protective kind of energy. And yes, that is part of our function as men in human society – to nurture and protect. It's not hard to imagine that a woman may have a deep genetically determined desire to have a man bonded to her who is dedicated to her protection and the protection of their children.

Although many men can identify easily with this type of love, we find it much harder to identify with the other side of our love: vulnerability. This is the energy within you which needs to be held, protected, and looked after. It's what you show of yourself when you open your heart to someone and meet them at a deep feeling level. That is the essence of male vulnerability.

Sadly, most men are not good at making themselves vulnerable or opening to the giving and receiving of love, except perhaps in the first flush of romance. You've probably heard it said that women want sex when they feel love for their man, while men need to have sex with a woman to feel their love for her. And there's truth in that. But why would men find being vulnerable so difficult, except during intercourse – and sometimes even then?

Perhaps the answer lies in society's expectations of men. Maybe our culture dictates that men should occupy the Warrior space rather than the Lover space. Maybe we learn that the Lover archetype and all the energies associated with it are the province of women rather than men. Perhaps boys are shamed by their peers and by society more generally if they show their vulnerability. Maybe at some level we expect boys to be tough and manly, to be more Warrior than Lover from Day One.

But we don't really need to know the answers to those questions to appreciate that all our lives would be more rewarding, gentler and more fulfilling if men were able to express their vulnerability and their need for love.

This is why men's groups can be so important for all of us – and by that I mean men, women and children alike. Why so?

I believe men fear judgement and criticism. It's an alien energy for us, one which destroys our confidence and power and diminishes our masculinity. There's something dark and shadowy about judgement and criticism. These are not energies helpful to us when we are trying to find our place in the world. These are not energies that we welcome in any way, as far as I can see. Yet judgements come at us from all sides.

A men's group which is free of judgement and criticism, which offers a sacred space where a man can open his heart and speak honestly and truthfully about who he is, allows a man to become softer and to enter more into his Lover. By doing so he may find his vulnerability and perhaps even embrace it, and so become a better husband, partner, lover, and father.

And that said, sex is very important for most men in a purely physical way. You might be a man who feels the drive to have sex so strongly that you want to fuck everything in sight. You might have a more modest sex drive. Strong sex drive or not, as a man you still carry the imperative to find a way of expressing this energy.

So powerful is this energy that it colours our thinking, encouraging us to mentally strip women as they walk past us in the street or to imagine, perhaps unwantedly, what it would be like to have sex with the female clerk in the store, or the waitress as she takes our order. Whatever our sexual orientation, the sexual imperative affects us all one way or another.

The path which beckons when we harbour these thoughts is a route to the sexual harassment and oppression of women. It's a path which reinforces the ambiguous attitude to sex in our society, where sex is shameful and we don't acknowledge our sexual urges, while at the same time we plaster sexualized images of women promoting perfume and consumer goods on every other billboard and TV advert.

Of course sex is a primal drive. There was a time when the survival of our species depended on high rates of reproduction, and so we men were gifted by evolution a high sexual drive fuelled by testosterone so we could reproduce as often as possible.

Natural though that may be, if you're walking down the street splitting people into categories according to your level of sexual interest in them, then your sexual energy is in control of you rather than the other way around. And if you're eyeing up women primarily as sexual objects rather than fellow human beings it's a fair guess you have some work to do on your sexual shadows.

In men's groups I've heard men speak of their fear around sexuality. A common theme seems to run through all of their stories: the fear of being seen as effeminate, feminine, weak, "a pussy", or unmanly. A man's fear of his Lover archetype, complete with its softness and tenderness, might alienate him from this softer yet extremely powerful side of himself.

Such is the force of our sex drive that it can cause us to make all kinds of decisions, both good and bad, about how to live our lives. Such is the force of the Lover that its urgings may seem irresistible, even when leading us into some self-destructive catastrophe.

A middle-aged man who leaves his wife and family for a woman twenty years his junior may be in the grip of forces he can't control, forces which may seem to offer instant gratification but which can damage him and others around him most profoundly. Perhaps he is unable to control the power of his Lover archetype and the sexual drive that lives there. He may be a man whose Sovereign is weak, a King unable to set the appropriate boundaries to curb his wounded Lover's seemingly irresistible wishes, impulses, needs and desires.

Instead, from his shadow unconscious, lover energy plays out in all kinds of dysfunctional behaviour, driving his life and denying him rational and conscious free choice in his life as a grown man.

We can all get more control over our Lover when we acknowledge the extraordinary power of this archetype and the amazing force it can have in our lives. Then we can begin to come to terms with it, and start dealing with all of the issues we have around sex, sexuality, intimacy, and above all our relationship to the feminine.

I believe a lot of the difficulties men have in these areas stem from the fact that many of us have an ambivalent relationship with the feminine, either external or internal. Many men I work with seem to be in awe of the feminine, even fearful of it. Many men seem never to have fully separated from Mother and identified fully with the world of the masculine. And it hardly needs to be said that a powerful sex urge combined with a deep-seated fear of the feminine, whether that be conscious or unconscious, is not going to produce a happy outcome for anyone.

And what of porn?

Boys as young as ten are now accessing porn on the Internet. This is their first introduction to sex generally and more particularly to the way we "make love". How will that impact their relationships with real women later in life? That's a question only time will answer.

It's an important question, though, since the majority of men in the world today, at least in the Western world, are taking advantage of the easy availability of porn on the Internet to relieve their sexual desires quickly and simply.

Unfortunately this plays right into a male tendency to objectify women and make them into sexual objects. I suspect it will also make many men less interested in genuinely "making love" to a woman. More than anything else, porn allows us to reach inside ourselves and express our sexual desires, no matter how shadowy and dark they may be. This hardly seems like a healthy process, certainly not when compared to healing your sexual shadows and fully owning your mature masculine sexuality.

You may even have reached a point where you prefer Internet sex to real sex with a real person. After all, it's easier, it's quicker, and it can certainly seem simpler. But this form of sexual self-expression denies you the deep emotional connection and satisfaction which can come from fully experiencing your male power and potency during lovemaking.

I've worked with men who have sexual issues for many years, and in that time I've watched men discover how to fully embody and embrace their masculinity during lovemaking. If you take the potentially challenging path of doing this, you'll move well beyond the transient pleasure of simply fucking. And as you do that, you'll discover all the rich and delicious experiences your body can provide you with in the Lover archetype.

When your Lover is alive and well, and you're on good terms with it, the world changes in a beautiful way. You find yourself caring about things you never imagined would matter to you: the aesthetics of your environment, the way you look after yourself, your appreciation of beauty and the Natural World. And, of course, when you're living in harmony with your internal Lover, the quality of your relationships will improve, whether sexual or otherwise.

The Lover In Harmony With Other Archetypes

The Lover is what humanizes all of our other archetypes. Without the Lover we can be detached, unfeeling, perhaps even inhumane. The Lover holds our compassion, our capacity to empathize, and our ability to feel for others: all vital elements of our humanity. To fully enjoy life we all need a balanced psyche where the power of the Lover archetype and its liking for sensuality is contained and boundaried by the power of the King, the Warrior, and the Magician.

So the Lover needs boundaries. In particular he needs boundaries set by his King, because those are the boundaries that provide a structure within which the Lover's energy can flow in a controlled and contained way. Without these boundaries a man's lover energy can be all-consuming and self-destructive.

The Lover also needs the energy of the Warrior, who can exercise the clean cut where something has come to an end and needs to be removed from your life – the ending of a relationship being a prime example of this. The Warrior's energy is needed to cut through old ties which might continue to entangle the Lover, for he hesitates to make a clean break for fear of the grief which may follow.

And the Lover requires the detachment of the Magician so he can step back into a more detached and objective place from where he can see the bigger picture and get in touch with the true reality of life.

The Emotional Wound in the Lover Quarter

To cut to the chase, the cause of the wound in this quarter is a lack of love and connection – or a loss of love and connection – in childhood. More broadly, it's about your emotional needs not being met during childhood. And because this archetype is so primal, so fundamental to us, deep and painful Lover wounds can still be inflicted on us during adolescence, maybe even into early adulthood.

I see a lot of men and women on my workshops still carrying the grief and pain of the loss of their grandparents, especially when these were the kindest and most loving adults in their life.

I work with many others who were wounded in the sensitive area of the Lover by the unthinking (or deliberate) cruelty of disciplinarian teachers, unfeeling parents, and jealous siblings.

One of the most common causes of a Lover wound in men (and women, for that matter) seems to be the pain of abandonment – whether that abandonment was real or simply an interpretation of events by the child. This is especially true among those who were sent away to boarding school during childhood. This wound, always damaging, but worst in those men who were sent away to boarding school without explanation at the age of 7 or so, has seared the souls of generations of fathers and sons in countries where this kind of education was seen as a privilege. For those with a personal interest in this area, the work of Nick Duffel and his group Boarding School

Survivors may be very helpful (you can find it online).

Wounds in this archetype can be especially painful to sensitive boys who need respectful care, love and support as they grow and develop. We are all born with different degrees of resilience; what wounds one boy may leave another untouched.

The sensitivity of boys – as described by the men they have become, the men I work with, men who are still carrying the pain of childhood abandonment or betrayal of love and trust, the pain of the loss of significant adults, siblings and pets, the destructive impact of harsh words or humiliation by their peers, the damage caused by a mother or sisters who smothered a boy with love and made him dependent on feminine approval, indeed each man with his own unique story of wounding – yes, the sensitivity of boys never ceases to astound me. No wonder so many men carry wounds in this archetype.

Whatever the cause of a boy's Lover wound, the outcome is the same: he somehow comes to believe he's not lovable, or that there's something wrong with the way he loves, or that he's incapable of loving others, or some variation of this theme.

As always it makes no difference to the child's view of himself that the real problem lies with other people: bad, unfeeling, unloving, insensitive, inadequate or unwilling parents, peers, siblings, teachers, priests, carers and other adults… and of course the wider society which looks the other way.

Children don't usually think that way. They almost always take emotional wounding as somehow being their fault. The logic in a child's mind, consciously or unconsciously, goes like this: "They wouldn't be treating me like this unless I deserved it. There must be something about me which made this happen. It's my fault. There's something wrong with me." This is because almost all children idealize their parents, even when their parenting is totally inadequate.

You probably have a Lover wound if these words resonate, sound familiar, or the patterns of your relationships make you wonder if you carry any of these beliefs: "I'm not lovable." "There's something wrong with the way I love." "I don't love right." "I can't love." "I don't know how to love properly." And such like.

Whatever the cause of your original Lover wound, the beliefs about yourself which grow from it will interfere with your ability to give and receive love as an adult in an open-hearted, trusting, and truly connected way. These beliefs are expressed in adult life in statements such as: "No-one will ever want me." "I will never have a successful relationship." "Women don't find me attractive." "I haven't met anyone good enough." "I just haven't met the right woman yet." You may know some others.

So if you repeatedly have relationships which fail, if you've never been in a long term relationship, if you just can't seem to find the right woman (or man), if you're still searching for some ideal vision of femininity, if you are overly dependent on a woman to be happy, and especially if you feel you're still in the sway of the feminine, then you most likely have some form of Lover wound.

Mind you, we all have this wound to some degree. It's simply not possible for parents to meet any child's needs perfectly. The question is – were our parents *loving enough*? Did they meet enough of our needs to give us a sense of security and trust in ourselves, and equally important, in the people around us... and even, perhaps, trust in the world?

I am told that Balinese children are some of the most secure, confident and happy children in the world. (Apparently the adults generally look much happier than people in the West, too.) Maybe that has something to do with the way the Balinese care for their babies, which is very different to our Western approach.

Balinese people regard babies and young children as sacred beings because they are so close to the beginning of this life and also their previous past life. In fact the Balinese believe that children are in the realm of the gods and have the ability to see the supernatural world. And so from birth until the age of three months babies are carried everywhere and are never placed on the ground, just as befits a little god.

The traditional way of raising children in Bali involves the whole family including aunties, uncles, grandparents, great grandparents, cousins, nieces and nephews, and even the more distant family members. Men, women and children of all ages adore babies. Parents let complete strangers pick up and hold their babies. The effect this has is quite extraordinary: Balinese children appear to be some of the most secure anywhere in the world. How many of us in the West would even consider raising our kids like this? We tend to see baby-care as more about what is possible for us than what our babies might need.

We saw earlier how the Lover wound is a primal wound: a baby emerges from its mother's body to be greeted either with complete love and acceptance or with something different, something less. Sure, nothing in life is 100% one way or the other, and so it is for the Lover wound: there are degrees of acceptance, love and connection.

Perhaps the extreme is where a baby is both unplanned and unwanted when it arrives, a state of being which must inevitably be communicated to the child by the mother's and father's energy. And even for a baby who is wanted, cherished and adored there will be times when the Lover connection with mother or father (or someone else) fractures or breaks. After all, parents are incapable of meeting the unbounded demands of their children all of the time in all the ways that the child needs.

No matter that a wounding disconnection may be caused by the parents' tiredness or exhaustion, lack of emotional intelligence, or simple incapacity to love. Any lack of love, any break in connection, is something the child will most often believe is his or her fault. The pain of such loss can be intense; so intense it may seem to be life-threatening. If it is not grieved appropriately, the pain remains unprocessed, shoved away in the shadow bag perhaps, waiting to strike with any future loss which evokes the memory.

And so the Lover wound becomes part of a boy's self-image. Possibly consciously, more likely unconsciously, he comes to believe certain things about himself. "I can't love right." "I'm not lovable." "Nobody loves me." "There's something wrong with the way I love."

These self-beliefs may keep him away from deep connection and the joy of loving truly, madly, deeply in the future. After all, why risk a repetition of the pain of the loss of connection with someone you loved so dearly? Better even, to find a reason to break a relationship off before getting too deeply involved. And so every failed relationship, every broken romance, and every lost opportunity to truly connect with others later in life may be the result of the Lover wound in childhood.

Remember, too, that the Lover wound can stem from any significant loss: losing a parent to death or divorce, grandparents dying, close friends moving away, pets dying, moving house, moving to a new home, being sent away to school, a new baby brother or sister arriving and the loss of the parents' love and attention which may follow... all these losses, and many more, may leave a child wondering "What did I do to cause this?" Each and every loss may wound him again in the Lover quarter. How much better, then, never to trust in love again than to experience the pain of loss once more.

Lover wounds produce grief at the very least. And grief is a burden that weighs a man or woman down, destroying vitality and preventing access to joy, until floods of tears are shed to relieve that burden. Even in adulthood a loss of any kind can have a major impact on a man who was wounded in the quarter of the Lover as a child, for such loss can evoke the energy of an earlier wound and reconnect a man to his repressed pain and unexpressed grief.

There are many reasons to grieve, but some are subtle. Tangible losses are easy to understand. Less obvious is the pain associated with something you never had, for this can be a powerful loss too: the loss of innocence in a childhood afflicted by abuse, the loss of the chance to be a parent, the loss of good health, the loss of youth, the loss of virility as age advances... yes, losses come in many forms. Fortunately for us all, bringing grief out of shadow and shedding tears for your losses is possible no matter how long ago you were wounded.

When lover energy goes into shadow it can either inflate or deflate.

The Inflated Shadow: The Addict, The Needy One

Because it is so primal and powerful, when lover energy goes into shadow it can be very destructive.

Inflated, shadow lover energy generates many types of addictions. These addictions include drugs, porn, alcohol, sex, food, emotional neediness and dependency – all intense emotional experiences for the wounded part of a man. These experiences can be a way of "feeling alive", of soothing the pain of the Lover wound, or a route to numbing the pain of the loss which lies at the core of that wound.

A man in the grip of his addicted Lover may become lost in the overwhelming experience of sensations, impressions and information coming at him from the outside world.

Anything that hints at his wound can trigger an emotional reaction which absorbs him completely. He can get drawn into a reaction to almost any event in his life. An angry word from a lover can send him into despair. A seductive look from a woman he happens to chance across in a bar can seem like salvation. The scent or beauty of a flower can overwhelm him. Hearing a chance word or a line of a song evocative of something he lost (or never had) may plunge him into a waterfall of tears.

This loss of awareness about the limits of his own emotionality, this loss of boundaries, is very clear in the way that the inflated Lover craves the next high, the next drink, the next cigarette, the next orgasm. These are the things which the addict loves, oblivious of balance, oblivious of his own needs, and oblivious of his own power to extract himself from this situation.

Even men who constantly return to situations which are harmful – for example, a relationship which oscillates between harmony and violence – are displaying some sort of addiction to this experience. The emotionality of such experiences seems to somehow fulfil their expectations of life, or perhaps gives them a sense of being alive.

People in the grip of addiction are unable to escape the agony and ecstasy of the circular path between addiction and release. They cannot extract themselves from the Lover complex. The Sovereign is off-line, the Warrior has gone to sleep, and the Magician has lost his power to reason with them.

At its heart this is all about the experience of sensuality, the desire to experience the next amazing high at the expense of anything in the longer term.

This is not the mania of the grandiosity and sense of unlimited power of the inflated Sovereign. The inflated Lover is much more about something that was lost or something that never was, and the resulting need, narcissism and confusion.

The root of that narcissism is a search for anything that will ease the pain of the unfelt and unexpressed grief that eats away at a man's soul. The paradox here is that grieving, allowing the tears to fall, is not painful; quite the opposite – it is relieving, in fact. In fact, as far as I'm aware, there is no other way to deal with the pain of unexpressed grief than to allow the tears to fall. The impact of doing so is remarkable, for tears almost always open the way to joy.

Yet people avoid shedding their tears because they think the process will be painful beyond measure, that they will fall into their ocean of grief and drown. So the addictive cycle continues: anything which offers apparent relief, no matter how temporary, is seized upon, only to be inevitably followed by an even clearer and perhaps even heightened experience of grief. That in turn requires some form of consolation, of relief, and so the cycle continues.

The inflated Lover appears to be seeking a resolution of his addiction to sensuality by searching continuously, as Robert Moore and Douglas Gillette put it, for "the ultimate and continuous high". This is why "he rides from village to village, from adventure to adventure, and from one woman to another." Yet each time he's confronted with mortality, weakness and limitations; then his dream is shattered, and so once again "he saddles his horse and rides out looking for a renewal of his ecstasy."

At the root of all such addictions is the Lover wound – a belief that you are not worthy of receiving love, perhaps, or that somehow you are unlovable, or there's something wrong with the way you love, or love is something you can't understand or will never receive. As we've seen, this wound stems from disrupted connections at an early age: a connection never formed with mother, or a connection formed and broken, perhaps. A family which broke up, or a loved one who died. All of those possibilities, and more.

Maybe the addiction is an attempt to soothe the unexpressed pain, or perhaps it represents an attempt to return to the unboundaried state of connection with something loved and lost. In either case, it can be all-absorbing. The world becomes a stage on which the inflated Lover can act out his needs. Everything is about him and his needs. Unfortunately, the audience often fails to appreciate the wounded Lover's performance, especially when they've seen it day after day.

Lover wounds can show themselves at any stage of life. I recently worked with a man who'd made a choice between two women, and later came to believe he'd married the wrong one. He tormented himself with thoughts of the ecstasy that might have followed had he only made the correct choice.

Such pain. Such pain. Yet all he needed to resolve his pain was to find a place where he could grieve the choice he *didn't* make and so let go of the possibilities about what may have followed if he had made that choice – all of which were, of course, mere fantasy in his mind. His grieving slayed the demon of over-connectedness to the lost loved one and restored the man's own boundary.

In doing this work in the safety of the "container" created in an Emotional Process Work workshop he also reached his original wound – absence of connection with his mother, an unstable and angry woman whom he believed had never wanted him. His inner little boy's ardent desire to connect with Mother and receive her love was manifested in his idealized vision of this woman in his adult life. When he let go of her, he went a long way to healing his mother wound, too.

Many adult men find themselves overwhelmed in the presence of strong feminine energy. Some of these men are still invested in their childhood attachment to mother. Others have never let go of the feminine so they can identify with the masculine. And some haven't yet developed masculine ego structures which form an internal boundary around the feminine. Men in these situations can all too easily be overwhelmed by the unconscious forces of the inner and outer feminine.

A man may carry an unconscious desire to return to the state of connectedness with mother that he once experienced as bliss, where mother was like the Almighty. Underlying this is a lack of clear boundaries around his sense of self. This induces a kind of worship of women, a dependency on having connection with them, a despair when each relationship ends and an elation when the next one forms.

Addiction to repeated emotional entanglement with the feminine characterized by loss of a sense of self and emotional neediness then follows naturally. Addiction thrives when a man does not have clear internal boundaries which define who he is.

Sex addiction, porn addiction, compulsive or inappropriate sexual behaviour – all of these can be an expression of lover energy which was put into shadow and has since emerged in a darker, more shadowy form. (Robrt Bly memorably suggested that what is put into shadow "de-evolves towards barbarism".)

Sexual kinks such as bondage and sexual humiliation may originate in a psychic need to try and control the power of the feminine. Men who enjoy these pastimes report how satisfying they feel. It's all about their ability to control, to feel power. Such power may indeed feel like poetic justice for those who were powerless against the force of the feminine during childhood.

Many of these dynamics hint at an inadequate separation from the feminine and a lack of identification with the masculine. This can leave a man in a state of confusion, if not fear, in the face of the feminine: fear of being absorbed, fear of not knowing who he is, fear of co-dependency. And at the same time, he may feel (or more likely not even be aware of) an unconscious attraction to the feminine because of his innate knowledge of how delicious and sensual unification with the feminine can be. The baby at the breast is indeed in unity with mother... safe, warm, blissful.

This confusion, this fear, is repressed into the unconscious so a man can attempt to live life as a seemingly independent adult in the world. But as always with the shadow, repressed thoughts and feelings do not lose their energy; they simply leak out in unexpected and unwanted forms which continue to influence a man's sexuality, masculinity, and ability to love cleanly.

Make no mistake about it, any loss can produce grief, and sometimes this can inflate to unreasonable levels. Regrettably the needs expressed by a man in the grip of the Shadow Lover are, quite literally, inexhaustible and impossible to meet.

Anyone – man or woman – who is rash enough to try and meet them will quickly discover that what they offer can never be enough, nor good enough, to fill the void which lies inside the inflated Lover. Co-dependency is a natural result, and will continue until one or other party realizes there is a better way of life than to be trapped in this dynamic.

This is the extreme form of the inflation in this quarter, but there are many other ways in which the inflated Lover will make himself felt. Emotional neediness, clinginess, the sense you may have of being in a relationship with a child rather than an adult, the endless demands for time and attention, the narcissism of someone whose needs occupy all the space in a conversation or relationship, the sense that you don't matter: these are the signs you're around an inflated Lover with an insatiable need for connection.

The Deflated Shadow: The Stoic

The opposite pole of the shadow is the deflated Lover. Since this archetype is all about the energy of life and vitality, it's probably not going to surprise you to read that when the Lover deflates, life may become dull, unemotional, perhaps even tedious.

There is a monotony and flatness in the emotional experience of a man in this place. He simply can't feel his joy. Mind you, he can't feel much at all. But this is different to the lack of feeling and emotional detachment of the Magician.

The Lover's lack of feeling is a symptom of him stepping out of the flow of life. Chronic depression and a sense of being cut off from himself is the defence against feeling of the deflated Lover. The defence is against feeling anything real, which seems to be so painful that even lack of vitality may be more appealing than the pain of feeling.

This deflation can also manifest as stoicism: a lack of emotion, a lack of sexual interest, a lack of sensual awareness and sensitivity. This stoicism can grow into withdrawal, depression, and even a loss of interest in life itself.

Sometimes, of course, the poles switch, and the Lover shadow can take a man from this place into a kind of maniacal search for feeling, for something to live for, for something which satisfies his need to feel sensual.

How To Be Truly Alive In Your Lover Energy

In their book *King Warrior Magician Lover* Robert Moore and Douglas Gillette stated that the Lover archetype was the most inadequate, most repressed archetype in men. They wrote that in 1990. They were almost certainly wrong then. They are definitely wrong now. The most stunted and undeveloped archetype in men today is the Sovereign.

In fact the 1980s was a decade which saw the development of considerably *more* lover energy in men, albeit in an unbalanced form. For that was the decade of the "New Man", a popular concept among both men and women. For a while, anyway.

The New Man was a man who rejected sexist attitudes and traditional male roles (whatever those may have been!) in favour of a caring, sensitive and non-aggressive nature and a willingness to meet women on their own ground. This was a popular concept in the 1980s, particularly with women, perhaps because new men were supposed to take responsibility for their share of childcare, cooking, and cleaning.

Nowadays parents who naturally split childcare between them might find this idea strange. Many strongly masculine fathers expect to look after their kids these days. But back in the 1980s male roles had been defined along the lines of "provider" and "worker" for a long while. Then in the 1990s traditional heavy-duty male jobs such as mining, shipbuilding and construction declined rapidly in the western world with jobs being exported to developing countries in very large numbers. Traditional male roles were very much in flux, perhaps even under attack.

Many men found themselves disempowered and lacking a clear sense of identity because of this shift. So perhaps becoming more Lover oriented, or if you prefer softer and more feminine, was a natural response. Or perhaps what was really happening was simply the disempowerment of men. Whatever the origins of the shift in male identity which gave birth to the idea – and the reality – of the New Man, the end point certainly wasn't popular with women, who very quickly found that "New Men" didn't match up to what they really wanted in the masculine.

What went wrong was not the development of the Lover archetype in men but the weakness or even absence of Warrior and Sovereign. Certainly a lot of the territory men were exploring in those days – childcare, sensitivity, awareness of feelings and such like – is now widely accepted as part of a man's life and relationship.

What seems to be the real problem around masculinity, a problem we still face today, is a decline in the energy of Warrior and Sovereign. While there's nothing wrong with Lover energy in men, it needs to be matched by a capacity to be firm (i.e. to form boundaries and be resolute) when that's what is needed.

Should you feel the need to develop your Lover energy, here are some suggestions. Remember that your Lover is both the source of your ability to connect with others and your access point to the expression of grief. And that, strange as it may seem, is the route to joy.

1 Be Sensual

First of all, get in touch with the Lover within you by fully engaging with everything your senses have to offer you and simply taking more time to really enjoy the things which bring you pleasure.

You can do this in simple ways: increasing the time, attention and energy you put into connecting with nature, enjoying the taste of good food or wine, savouring the glorious experience of making love, and enjoying other sensual experiences such as having a massage.

And you could, for example, schedule time to be with your partner or children, making sure that you are fully present with them so you can truly share the experience. You might also choose to spend time with yourself or indulge your own inner child in some way.

Being sensual means appreciating what your senses offer you, and being fully open to receive and enjoy those sensual experiences.

2 Be Open To Healing Work

Being fully present in your life is an important way to moderate the endless cycle of using external events or substances to feel better. However, as any addict can testify, it's not a remedy for the Lover's pain and neediness. Sure, going out for a gourmet dinner and savouring every bite may be a sensual experience which puts you more in touch with your lover energy, but to move comfortably in and out of your Lover archetype *by choice,* you will certainly need to heal the emotional wounds which lie deep in your shadow unconscious.

This is the province of the wounded inner child. And every single one of us carries, to a greater or lesser degree, wounds in our inner child. Perhaps some of these wounds are so early and so profound that they cannot be completely healed. But unless you do some work on them they may continue to run your life for ever.

In fact you can pretty much assume that any issues you may have with addictions, neediness, excessive stoicism, endless grief, poor relationships, lack of self-love, inability to love others, inability to play, and a lack of joy in your life (among other challenges), require two things.

First, you could do some healing work on the emotional wounds of your inner child. Second, you might like to find ways to develop a strong internal Sovereign who can hold the wounds of your inner child. These are, after all, wounds in your Sovereign's Kingdom and you, as Sovereign, are responsible for holding them.

This is essential, I believe, because some inner child wounds seem to be too primal, too deep or too early to ever be healed completely. While the pain can be soothed with Emotional Process Work, sometimes what's also needed is an internal parent or leader – the Sovereign in you – who is strong enough to hold that part of yourself and comfort it.

If you feel your energies in these areas are out of balance you can work on your emotional wounds in appropriate workshops and bring them back to a healthy balance, especially around the development of Sovereign energy. You can see more details of these possibilities in the resources section of this book.

3 Dive Into Your Shadow

Are you ready to dive into your shadow unconscious to explore what happened to you in your early years, and to do the essential work of reparation and healing? Are you willing to do this for your own sake and for the sake of your loved ones?

It may mean diving into the ocean of grief inside you to mourn your losses – not only the things you had, but also the things you never had but desperately needed (unconditional love, for one).

It may mean some therapeutic work on the inadequate parenting or lack of love that you experienced in childhood.

It may mean healing the wounds of loss and separation.

Many of us know the painful experience of significant people dying during our childhood, or of being separated for some reason or another from those we loved, long before we were old enough to cope with that experience. (Boarding school "survivors" are well acquainted with such experiences.) And even when we were older we may still have experienced losses from which we have never recovered because we have never grieved.

Your sensitivity, sensuality and compassion as well as your ability to connect with others, with yourself and with Planet Earth all reside in the Lover quarter. So to be fully present in any relationship, to be fully present in your life, and to be able to give and receive love freely, sure in the knowledge that you can love others and they can love you in return, you may well need to do some healing work in your Lover archetype.

And given that you're prepared to do this deep work, all the other aspects of your Lover archetypal energy will become more powerful and profound. Your life will seem brighter, richer and more colourful, more stimulating and joyous, more of a life to be lived.

4 Indulge Your Sensitivity

The Lover within you is very sensitive and needs to feel the "softer" things in life for you to experience your humanity fully. First and foremost among these is a sense of connection and love, or appreciation and affection, from others. Find these and you feed your Lover. However, there are many more ways to give the Lover within what he needs.

You might choose, for example, to listen to beautiful music that moves you, to dance to joyous music that energizes you, to cry to sad music that helps you touch your grief and start to mourn your losses.

You might choose to arrange a surprise date with your partner, wife or girlfriend, or bring her flowers. You might choose to write her (or him) a love letter or simply to tell her that you love her truly, madly, deeply. After all, those things are what the Lover inside all of us wants to see, hear, and experience.

If you know a young baby whose needs are being met and who is truly loved try this: next time you see the child, cuddle him or her and see how this feels. You may feel his or her innocence and purity and you may sense the baby's connection to something bigger than himself. The same energy remains within you to this day and it needs to be taken care of.

5 Emulate Others Who Embody The Lover's Qualities

You may find it helpful to emulate men whom you admire and who embody the qualities you wish to develop in your own life. You can watch films and read biographies of these men (and women) to learn more about the qualities you would like for yourself.

But what if all of this emotional "stuff" doesn't come naturally? Well, this is probably a great opportunity to practice the old adage: "fake it till you make it". Simply act passionately, act with enthusiasm, act as though you already know what it means to be truly sensual. Show your emotions as if you are really feeling deeply. Go to concerts and really listen to the music. Study art with enthusiasm and passion. Enjoy a sudden, unexpected embrace with your lover, partner or wife. Play uninhibitedly and enthusiastically with your kids. Taste and savour every morsel as you eat. Dance like your life depended on it. Make love as though you were going to die tomorrow. In other words, simply be passionate about your life and all that it offers. For, as David H Wagner says in his book *Backbone: The Modern Man's Ultimate Guide to Purpose, Passion and Power*, "The Lover loves what he loves, but he wants to love it hard."

6 Learn To Love Your Inner Child - And All Your Other Parts Too!

How often have you heard the words, "Love yourself"?
Surely, that shouldn't be too difficult?
Sadly, it all too often is.

The problem is that many of us internalized a model of love from our parents that was less than perfect. A model of love that may have ranged from good through adequate to downright inadequate, unkind and uncaring, none of which remotely represent unconditional love.

The way you were parented as a child in the world by mum and dad is likely to be the way you now look after your own inner child. So if parental love wasn't big in your childhood you may need to learn how to love your own inner child more freely, which is essential for good emotional health. Doing so will certainly make you a better father if or when you have children of your own to parent.

Start by imagining what a real child in the world wants – mostly, attention, affection, love and respect.

If you can give those qualities to your own inner child, perhaps by spending a few minutes every day talking to him, he'll soon respond by blossoming into an active part of your personality. Unfortunately that can lead to endless trips to the adult equivalent of the sweet shop or candy store, together with self-indulgence on a grand scale and a lack of responsibility as well. So what you'll need to do then is to start setting clear and firm boundaries around the behaviour of your own inner child. You'll only be able to do this if you carry sovereign energy strong enough to hold those boundaries.

On a practical level your inner child is the source of your innocence, your fun, your play and your laughter, not to mention your sexuality and sensuality. Looking after this part of your inner world is vitally important to your well-being as a man who can enjoy a long and happy life. If you don't know how to look after your inner child, how to love him, hold him, and bless him, I strongly recommend that you get some help. For example, take part in a workshop where these things are explained, demonstrated, and made real.

Of course, loving yourself isn't only about loving your inner child; it's also about loving *all* the parts of yourself.

Many people carry a harsh inner critic which manifests as self-denigration, lack of self-care, even self-harm in the more extreme forms.

You might be overtly self-harming in some physical way. But self-harming also includes covert self-harming in the form of behaviours such as eating too much, not getting enough exercise, drinking too much, taking drugs, not getting enough sleep, staying in abusive relationships, and eating things that aren't good for you. In either case it would most likely be helpful to have a look in your shadow bag to see what might be behind this behaviour.

This work allows you to look at the parts of yourself which you pushed into shadow long ago – no doubt for some very good reason. You can get those parts of yourself out again and look at them in the light of today. You can explore your emotional wounds and Archetypal energies, heal them, restore balance, and so begin to fully express every aspect of yourself in all your power, magnificence and glory in the world.

And since how you look, your appearance, is a powerful symbol of self-love, you can do a few simple things right now to set out on the road to fully loving yourself. Start by simply caring for yourself better: dress better, groom yourself better, and be proud of your appearance and your environment.

The Boyhood Form Of The Lover Archetype: The Oedipal Child

All the boyhood archetypes are "immature" simply because the boy is the "immature" form of the man. However, these boyhood archetypes are essential to our development into a healthy and emotionally balanced adult man. They map out a natural pathway from boyhood to manhood. At the same time they are powerful and wonderful energies in their own right!

The boyhood form of the adult male Lover archetype is the Oedipal Child.

The Oedipal Child generates our passion, our wonderment, and our appreciation for the world around us – and the people in it. In its fullest expression this boyhood archetype has a deep sense of the oneness and interconnectedness of all things. Moore and Gillette suggested that the root of this energy is a sense of connectedness to Mother energy. As I understand it, this is not so much represented by a boy's real mother as by the idea of the Great Mother or the goddess Mother Earth, a nurturing mother seen in the myths and legends of many people over many cultures.

Sure, this is an idealized relationship which probably represents the idealized form of the connection between infant and mother after birth. But it is also a relationship which carries the essence of our spirituality, our connection with the world around us, and our relationship with Mother Earth. She takes the role here of the archetypal model of our ideal nurturing and supportive mother. At the same time our internal feminine archetype, our Anima, is mixed in with our vision of our own birth mother and the feminine energy in which she carried us and out of which she gave birth to us.

All men have to move away from the feminine so they can grow into, embrace and embody the masculine. This is, in fact, the work of every man, young or old, who wishes to grow fully into his masculine energy and live out his birthright as a man.

Unfortunately there are many men in our society who have, for one reason or another, never fully separated from "mother" in one form or another. These men may continually strive to reconnect deeply with the feminine or persistently search for the masculine world they intuitively know they should be inhabiting.

Challenging though this may be, it is not the whole story. For when a man carries the shadows of the Oedipal Child into adulthood, things can become really dysfunctional.

The Shadows of the Oedipal Child

As always, the shadows can manifest in inflated or deflated form.

The inflated shadow pole of the Oedipal Child is the Mummy's Boy. But why "Oedipal"?

As you might happen to know, Oedipus was a Greek king way back when who "accidentally" killed his own father, King Laius. It was quite understandable that Oedipus didn't recognize his dad, really, since Oedipus had been taken away from his family at birth and put on a hillside to die. Fortunately a shepherd rescued him and raised him to manhood. Unfortunately he was then able to fulfil his destiny and kill his father.

It's a long story how they got themselves into this pickle, but what it amounts to is that a prophet (a cunning Magician, no doubt) had told King Laius (a weak King, it would seem) that his own son, Oedipus, would grow up to kill him. Somewhat unsurprisingly Laius tried to prevent this by killing the boy first. However Oedipus, as we know, survived and killed dad instead.

Unfortunately events then took an even worse turn, because Oedipus somehow managed to marry his own mother, Queen Jocasta. Still, as Robbie Burns said, the best laid schemes "gang oft awry".

As you might easily imagine, things didn't go too well after this, particularly when the awful truth was uncovered. The Kingdom was blighted and Oedipus was eventually cast down.

It's an amusing legend, no doubt the kind of story the Greeks liked to tell each other, but for our purposes the real message comes directly from Freud's interpretation of the Oedipal myth: boys see their fathers as a rival for their mother's affections. And at some level boys want to remain firmly in the embrace of the feminine, a loving and glorious union we experience first in the uterus, and later at the breast.

If separation from mother and identification with the masculine (for which read Dad) doesn't happen, then the boy's inflated connection with the feminine and his perspective that mother is the goddess is only going to lead to him getting hurt.

You don't have to be a devotee of Freud's interpretation to see that there could well be truth in the general idea of a boy needing to give up the feminine and join the world of the masculine.

Moore and Gillette suggested that the Don Juan syndrome, a term they used to refer to a man's endless search for the perfect woman (really the immortal goddess), represents the inflated pole of the Oedipal Child, the Mummy's Boy, at work. He finds what looks like the ideal woman, then discovers she is flawed, casts her aside, and moves on to the next. He has not yet learned that perfection does not exist outside his unconscious mind.

Interestingly, they also suggested that heavy use of porn was an unconscious attempt to find the goddess among the endless parade of female bodies available in porn. Who knows if this is an interpretation too far, but there is a certain quality of softness – or perhaps more accurately a sense of his failure to fully embrace the masculine – in a man who's still inappropriately attached to the feminine during adulthood. He shows a reluctance, somehow, to do what it takes to form a truly mature relationship with a woman and step fully into the masculine world.

The other shadow pole of the Oedipal Child – the deflated pole – is the Dreamer.

This is a state of isolation, of self-absorption, of inactivity, and of relationships with intangible things such as ideas, dreams, concepts, and creativity. It looks like depression, but it could simply be another kind of search for unification with the idealized image of the feminine. Or perhaps this is another representation of the grandiosity of the Oedipal Child who seeks to possess mother completely so he can stay united with her for the rest of his life.

In Summary

The Lover archetype is the part of us that softens our Warrior with mercy, our King with compassion, and our Magician with tenderness.

The Lover's energy is primal, driving us to seek connection with others from the moment we are born. Unmet, unsatisfied, this desire for connection controls us with addictions and unboundaried desires.

We're all wounded here to some degree, and without a strong Sovereign to hold the boundaries in adulthood this archetype can rule our lives, sometimes with disastrous consequences.

The emotion associated with this archetype is grief; grief for what we had and lost, or what we should have had but was never present in our lives.

The healing work you may need to do for your Lover's wounding is to shed the tears of grief you've never expressed, and develop an internal Sovereign strong enough to care for and protect your own inner child.

Chapter 5

The Sovereign Archetype In Men: The King

Back in 1990 Robert Moore and Douglas Gillette suggested the most repressed archetype in men was the Lover. Whether this was ever true is open to debate. But nowadays one thing is certain: the most repressed, and ironically the most important, archetype in men is the Sovereign, or King.

The strength of your Sovereign archetype gives you the power and potency to be a powerful decision maker, the leader of your world, and the head of your Kingdom – whether that means your family, your business, the world over which you have influence, or simply your own life. Your sovereign energy is what makes you King in your own Kingdom.

Of course, women have a Sovereign archetype too: the Queen. She plays a similar role in the lives of women. But here we are looking at the masculine Sovereign archetype, the King.

When you read that your Sovereign is "head of your kingdom" you might think of something like the British monarch – an impressive ceremonial figure perhaps, but one without much power.

But the Sovereign archetype within you is certainly no mere figurehead; he is the part of you that leads you in all you do. He sets a vision, finds a purpose, and directs you towards it. He also establishes good relationships with the Kings and Queens around you, maintains order in your kingdom, and makes clear and fair decisions that benefit both you and all those for whom you're responsible.

Or at least he should do. But really, ask yourself, do you truly feel in control of your life in all areas? Few men seem to have a sense of running their own lives from a truly Adult, Sovereign place. In archetypal work I often hear men say they "feel like a child" (or a teenager) inside. Certainly a younger part of them seems very active in how they present themselves to the world.

And as you look around the world today, you may think there are few true Sovereigns of either sex. Certainly the world appears to lack balanced, authoritative, compassionate and wise leadership. That deficiency of sovereign energy can be seen at every level of society from governments all the way through to families. In families it seems the powerful, potent and compassionate wisdom of a strong father or grandfather is rare today. What's gone wrong with our society, then, that we have so few true Sovereigns, so few true Kings, in the world of the masculine?

In part I believe this lack of sovereignty has come about because there are so few rites of passage in our lives.

A rite of passage is an event recognized by a culture or a tribe as a transition from one stage of life to another. This includes male initiation rituals, which have a powerful impact on boys and young men because they speak to a deep, ancestral part of the male psyche.

These rituals mark a transition from boyhood to manhood, young Hero to mature Warrior, Warrior to Elder, and so on. They demonstrate beyond any doubt what's expected of a boy by the men, the leaders, and the Elders in his society. They show him that he's now a member of the tribe, a member of the kingdom. That is his privilege; in return his sacred duty is to obey the rules and assume his responsibilities.

Rites of passage also trigger a man's emotional development as he moves from one stage of life to another. They help him grow up; in fact, they appear to be essential if he is to become a mature man in his society.

In the West we rarely find such rites of passage nowadays. Even so they persist as cultural echoes, as rituals and events which somehow look – or feel – like a rite of passage: getting your first driving licence, making love to someone else for the first time, joining the military, getting your first job, getting married, the birth of your first child, the death of grandparents, the death of your parents, and so on, and so on.

Yet important though such things may be, they are not really transformative events in the way that rites of passage are. True rites of passage have a powerful effect on men, causing something in the male psyche to "switch on", to open up a whole new level of psychological development so the brain starts working in a new way.

Nowadays, Emotional Process Work and Shadow Work may fulfil some of the functions of ancient rites of passage. These workshops offer men and women an opportunity to gain some healing and open up the developmental steps which were missing from their lives as they grew up.

I've seen people grow before my eyes as they experience the power of using their Sovereign archetype to plan and control their lives. I've seen them learn how to assert themselves by accessing their Warrior energy so they can bring order where there was previously chaos. I've seen them shed the grief they carry in their Lover over unmourned losses and step into their joy as a result. I've seen them overcome blocks and work through belief systems and behaviours that hold them back in life by accessing their Magician archetype and finding out what is really controlling their behaviour.

These workshops hold the possibility of transformation because they help people step into a new identity or a new way of living with a more mature, more evolved sense of self.

However, the absence of significant rites of passage in our society isn't the whole story behind the weakness – even absence – of the King archetype in men in Western society.

Before we go on, consider the kind of qualities the Sovereign archetype embodies: integrity, authenticity, wisdom, discernment, justice, compassion, clarity, potency, power, vision, mission, strength, humility… How do such things grow in us?

Boys have to learn how to be men; beyond that, they have to learn how to be mature men, how to step into their kingship. And this seems to happen when they're brought up surrounded by other men who've already made that transition: mature middle-aged men, fathers, mentors, wise Elders and grandfathers, and other male role models.

So if boys – and young men for that matter – have no fathers, Elders, or mentors who embody the energy of the mature King and who can demonstrate in every moment what it means to be a Sovereign, how are they ever to learn the meaning of sovereignty, leadership, self-control, and self-determination for themselves?

Sadly, most of them don't, and society pays the price.

Young men carry a profound desire for connection with mature male energy. Just as boys crave closeness and connection with their fathers, so young men (and, to be honest, a great many men in their

30s and 40s too) crave the experience, the presence, the energy, and the wisdom of older men. They can't articulate this – it's a deeply felt craving for something their soul knows they need and never had.

One of the older men who staffed my workshops a few years ago – sadly he has since died – was, without doubt, a cantankerous old man who irritated many of his peers. But, mysteriously, on every workshop there were always young men clustered around him, seeking his advice and counselling or simply enjoying his presence.

Why? Because in some way he embodied the kind of wise Elder energy which these young men instinctively knew they needed.

Such fatherly, supportive energy provides the kind of intimate emotional connection with masculinity that leads boys and young men to a true understanding of what it means to be a mature man, a King. By example, a mature masculine man can show younger men how to be with a woman in the way women desire. In fact, being around men who embody the sacred masculine provides a young man with a firm foundation for every aspect of his own masculinity. To put it another way, that is why male mentoring is essential for every young man.

Yet our tragedy is that so few of our young men, who so desperately crave this support, this experience of being around men, this primal feeling of being among their own tribe, have men in their lives who are able to provide it.

Families may have no father present; and no matter how much she may try, a mother cannot instil the deeper meaning of masculinity into her boys. Or the father may be present, but know no more of such things than his sons, so the lack of embodied masculinity continues on from generation to generation.

Despite all of this, I've learned from my work with men who had no-one to show them the nature of sovereign energy as they grew up, that a young man's own King archetype is always there as a potential energy waiting to be accessed. I've seen how sports coaches, teachers, mentors, in fact any older man who has a consistent and positive influence on a young man's life, can provide a model of masculinity that a young man can internalize as a model of sovereign energy.

With this kind of male role model, a young man can learn how to develop his own leadership and kingly qualities. That's because simply being around wise and balanced older men who can pass on all kinds of male wisdom, including a felt sense of what it means to be a man, satisfies an instinctual need in younger men. This is the need to be appreciated, to be blessed, to be accepted as good enough, just the way they are.

It's a need that exists from boyhood all the way through to middle age. Surely you, like all other men, have experienced a time in your life when you desired the caring attention, love and support of an older man who could appreciate and accept you just the way you are?

Sadly, by early adulthood many of us have given up the conscious or unconscious hope of finding a mentor, an ally, a good father figure, a man strong in his Sovereign who can guide us into our own sovereignty. And so instead of blossoming into mature Kings, rich in wisdom and joy, appreciated and loved by the younger members of society, and by the citizens of our Kingdoms, men continue to live small lives, failing to display much of their true potency and power.

These are the men who become older men, not Elders. Perhaps that's why we have so many old people thrust into old folks' homes in what so often looks like an attempt to simply get them out of the way. Old people like this seem to have become a nuisance, not a respected resource. Ironic, really, since almost all of us will reach this age of transition. Hope for yourself that you develop into a true Elder, for then you may be acknowledged as such and gain the respect of those younger than yourself.

Important though all of this is, I believe there's another reason for the absence of true Kingship among men today: the emotional wound which blocks the development of sovereign energy in children, the wound of not being good enough. More of that in a moment.

If history tells us anything, it tells us that a society without good leaders, good Kings and Queens, and plenty of sovereign energy, is a society that will struggle to survive in the shorter or longer term.

Without the leadership of true Sovereigns, we are destined to experience lack of direction, lack of purpose, and lack of vision, for these are all the province of the King. This can lead to chaos, confusion, and ultimately the fall of the Kingdom.

Yet while all this may seem pessimistic and seems to paint a dark future for us, the wonderful news is that sovereign energy is latent within all of us. With the right support and training, and your own intention, you can step more and more fully into your own kingship and thereby transform your life.

The King In His Fullness

With that in mind let's look at the qualities of the mature King, the King in his fullness.

Ruling Well & Holding His Subjects' Projections

A King on whom the Sovereign's crown does not sit comfortably is a King who's not fully in his power.

Growing into that power is, at least in part, about being fully committed to your personal development and the healing of your emotional wounds. It's also about stepping up to face challenges, taking on leadership, and dealing with adversity. You could call this "working on yourself". True enough; the right kind of personal development work does produce maturity and, eventually, hard-won Kingship.

And, over the twenty-plus years I've been involved in the field of personal development, I've worked with a few young men who stood out as Princes. They have bags of sovereign energy in Shadow, so they don't embody sovereignty yet, but you can sense the kingship latent within them. Why are they so different? Who knows? Chance, circumstance, good genes, their emotional needs met as children? All of this, and more, no doubt. Fortunately, no matter what our genes or our background, we can pull sovereign energy out of shadow.

A Sovereign needs to be confident in his right to rule. He needs to embody the knowledge that he is in the right place, at the right time, doing the right thing. When he knows this, the people in his Kingdom will readily accept him as their Sovereign.

At the same time, the subjects look at their King and see in him their own repressed and denied qualities of sovereignty and kingship. This means a Sovereign must carry the projections of his people around leadership, sovereignty and kingship.

Unfortunately, while a King's subjects may project their golden shadows around sovereignty, their own positive but unexpressed qualities of leadership, onto him they may also start projecting negative qualities onto him. In our society, shooting down those who stand out from the crowd and ridiculing those who seek to embody their own kingship seem to be popular pastimes for those who lurk in the shadows of their own power.

Kings need to be able to hold this energy as well, ruling with balance and stability, compassion and wisdom, even when the projections which come flying at them are critical, judgemental, and negative. It's another aspect of the Sovereign's strength that he can hold this, not be affected by it, and still work for the benefit of his kingdom.

Authority, Power and Potency

When I think of a mature King in his fullness, I think of authority. I think of a respected ruler of a particular realm or kingdom. I think of the men I've looked up to in life, the ones who have modelled the qualities of integrity and authenticity which I aspire to bring more fully into my own life.

Nowadays our kingdoms may look more like our families, our businesses, our areas of influence, and the organizations which we serve. Yet even though we may not have a literal kingdom over which we rule, each and every one of us is – or should be – a Sovereign in our own realms.

Authority comes in many forms. Your authority as a mature King is the authority which comes from knowing yourself to be powerful and potent, from knowing how to use that power, and knowing how to lead with justice and wisdom. A mature King is strong and worthy of the respect of his citizens, his subjects, the people in his kingdom.

Such power and potency represent the outward expression of mature masculinity: this is seen in a man who knows who he is, what he is, what he stands for, and how to put his masculine energy out into the world in the most constructive way. He has a vision, a plan to execute it, and he knows his purpose in life. He also knows he is good enough just as he is.

To reach this state, he will almost certainly have done a lot of repair work on his own emotional wounds. These emotional wounds, untended and ignored as they are in most people, soak up a massive amount of innate energy, which is then not available as an expression of self in the world.

Most people spend a lot of time and energy defending against feeling their grief, their anger, their rage, their shame and other trauma. But to the extent that you are repressing these emotional wounds, so you are reducing the amount of energy you have available to express your power and potency in the world. And that means you are lessening not only your power and potency but also your authority in your kingdom.

If you are allowing your rage or your weakness to show up in the world, you will also be reducing the level of respect which your people will feel for you. This means you are less likely to be willingly accepted as a true Sovereign King who has a right to rule.

Reading this, it'll come as no surprise to you to learn that most respected and successful Kings have had to do a considerable amount of personal development work away from their Kingdoms to overcome emotional wounds in all of their archetypes. Only then can sovereign energy begin to come online in a clear and potent way.

Order and Stability

Being a Sovereign isn't just about authority. It's also about using that authority to maintain order and provide balance and stability. In a way the King is the individual who has the sign over his desk saying "The Buck Stops Here".

If the kingdom isn't functioning well, if the children aren't flourishing, if the employees are rebelling, if the business isn't prospering, whose responsibility is it, other than the King's?

To provide balance and stability to the kingdom, the King himself must be emotionally balanced and stable. This means he must understand himself, his weaknesses and strengths, the areas where he needs support, and the areas where he is strong. This emotional balance and stability allow the King to remain calm when challenges and adversity arise. They allow him to maintain a cool head, to work out what needs to happen next, and to make clear decisions for the benefit of all.

Those qualities can be particularly important when you're the King and you need to protect your realm. Whether the kingdom under threat is your family, business, company, organization, or something else, you need to know how to protect your subjects and yourself. You need to have sufficient clarity of mind and strength of purpose to respond appropriately when hostile or invading forces impinge on the boundaries of your kingdom.

That might mean an aggressive defence with warrior energy of what is yours by right. It might mean holding a parley of Kings using the counsel of your Magician to negotiate a settlement. It might mean a tactical retreat – a Warrior tactic. It might mean surrender, perhaps under the influence of the Lover. Whatever the outcome, you as King can earn the trust of your people by knowing what to do. That way, they will respect your right to rule.

However, that right to rule also depends on your ability to rule justly, with discernment and wisdom, and with compassion where appropriate. History shows that tyrannical kings who rule without any kind of compassion eventually fall victim to opposing forces, while a just and wise King is usually celebrated by his people.

Equally, a weak or abdicating King who allows himself to be swayed by minority factions can only expect the support of his subjects for a short time.

Of course, a mature King, a wise King, doesn't have to know all the options about how to defend the realm. He has three other archetypal energies to draw on. He has a Warrior on whom he can rely for strategy and tactics and, if needed, aggressive action against anyone who seeks to invade the kingdom or destroy it.

He also has a (hopefully) supportive Magician who can provide wise counsel, advice and information about possibilities. This allows the King to choose wisely between all the available options.

And he has a compassionate Lover who can remind him of the need to temper fierce action with loving energy. Throughout history this has been part of the Queen's role – to influence the King so he tempers his decisions with greater humanity.

In this way, the King is supported in making clear decisions for the benefit of the kingdom. Sure, the King sometimes needs to make hard decisions that serve the greater good or remove disruptive elements in his kingdom. Even so, all his actions are intended to ensure that the kingdom itself flourishes and continues to grow and develop, and to provide well for the majority of its citizens.

Holding His Wounds & The Wounds Of The Kingdom

Kings have always had to hold their kingdoms together in the face of famine, war, illness, invasion, and other natural and man-made disasters. I call this "holding the wounds of the kingdom". (Naturally, a King can also celebrate with his subjects when things are going well!)

On a personal level, the wounds of your kingdom might be illness within the family, financial misfortune, employment difficulties, or any of the other myriad of unexpected twists of fate and fortune which invariably assail us all in life. As King, you can hold these wounds until prosperity and good fortune return. You can also hold the wounds which afflict you personally, even as you continue ruling your kingdom with strength and wisdom.

If you are to hold, let's say, the wounds in your own Lover archetype you must have considerable strength in your Sovereign. Yet this is what a King is required to do: he must hold his own emotional wounds while tending to the "wounds" of the people around him too.

In the context of wounding, it's interesting to reflect on mediaeval Kings in Europe. Where a Prince, destined to rule from the moment he was born, was given every advantage, treated royally, mollycoddled even, and protected from the woundings which we all have to experience in life before we can grow, the result was almost always a weakling King who lasted but a short time on his throne.

This suggests that strength can come through adversity. I mean this in the sense that life will inevitably test us, wound us, and sometimes even overwhelm us with adversity. Yet our strength and our sovereignty can be forged in that crucible of adversity. It is where we learn the limits and possibilities of what we can do and the extent of the power we can exert.

Leaving A Legacy

A wise King doesn't rule simply for the present moment. A generative King, a King whose concern is for the wealth, well-being and productivity of his kingdom, plans ahead. To rule not just for the benefit of the current generation but also with forethought for future generations is a very sovereign act.

And in among that forward thinking and planning so characteristic of a Sovereign in his maturity and fullness comes another aspect of kingship or sovereignty: leaving a legacy.

Perhaps for women this is different, since their legacy is often their children. Men, however, seem to embody a desire to leave something tangible behind them, something beyond their children, when they die. Indeed, this often looks like their memorial on the Earth. Some men even seem to think that without leaving such a legacy their lives will have been pointless.

In its most grandiose form this desire to leave a legacy manifests as grand projects deliberately planned by a man as his own memorial. These may take the form of physical constructions of one kind or another, some of which scar the face of mother Earth. They may take the form of all-powerful business empires which for a time intrude on everybody's life and make themselves felt in every corner of our existence.

However, there are more useful legacies for men to leave behind: think of men like Martin Luther King, whose contribution to civil rights changed the course of history, or John F. Kennedy, who almost certainly prevented nuclear war between America and Russia in the 1960s.

Think of Nelson Mandela who led his people to freedom. Think of Shakespeare, who left a body of literature which is central to our understanding of the English language today, hundreds of years later. Think of Beethoven and Mozart, who left us with timeless music which soothes our souls. Think of the outstanding artists and creators of today, who may in time be remembered for their legacy of creation.

None of us need to aspire to such heights, though. For a man who dies sure in the knowledge that he fathered his children well and created a supportive family environment leaves an intangible legacy of huge importance.

Two Sovereign questions naturally come up at this point.

The first is simple: what will you be remembered for when you die?

The second is more personal and complicated: when you're on your deathbed, what will you remember as having made your life worthwhile? Will the things you achieved in your lifetime be truly significant for you?

Embodying A Vision For The Kingdom

I imagine we would all like to look back on our life from our deathbeds and be able to say that, yes, we lived a worthwhile life. Of course, this implies that throughout your life you had a vision of what your life, or more accurately the outcome of your life, should look like. Sadly, many men have no vision at all and run their lives from day to day, reacting to events in the moment rather than acting for the future.

If you don't have a vision for your life, perhaps something needs to change. If you're too busy looking after day-to-day issues and constantly responding to the demands others make on you with no time to think where you're going, then it's time to take a step back and start thinking more strategically.

I believe a vision for your life can emerge naturally from the greater maturity which comes from simply living your life. After all, life experience teaches us what we want and what is important to us. But how much better, how much more Sovereign, to spend time each year setting up and reviewing a vision for your Kingdom with goals for the short and the long term!

How can you do this? By simply taking the time and using the support of people who know how to vision. Do some research on the internet, buy a book on the subject, or check out the resources section of this book.

Inevitably, your vision of how your life will look will be shaped by what you believe about your life's purpose.

Life Purpose and Mission

When I speak of life purpose, which some people call "soul purpose", I'm talking about the reason you are right here, right now, on Planet Earth. Another way of looking at this is to see your life purpose as the way of spending your life which will give you a felt sense of living your "right life" and produce the greatest emotional and spiritual satisfaction.

As Sovereign, you also need a mission – this is the way you express your life purpose on a day to day basis. And by "mission" we don't mean something summed up in the kind of banal "mission statements" which so many companies have adopted in recent times.

As an example, one man on a recent workshop said his life purpose was "to create a world of love and connection by working with a strong open heart". His mission statement, the way in which he would fulfil his life purpose, was "I offer workshops in the countryside for children and adults in which I promote greater connection between men, women and children and the planet, and create greater awareness of how we are totally dependent on the well-being of Mother Earth for our survival."

You don't need to struggle with these ideas or try to fit them into someone else's format. Your vision for your life, your sense of purpose, and your mission are all entirely personal. The only thing which really matters is knowing what they are and how to achieve them.

So how do you find out? A man's early life (and sometimes his mid-life, too, perhaps up the age of fifty) is often a time of experimentation, of finding out what the deeper purpose behind his existence might be. Sure, there's a presumption here, and not a small one, either: that there is indeed a higher purpose behind our existence, our very presence on the planet. You can take that idea or not as you choose. What's certain is that not all men have a sense of their life purpose or their mission. But all true Kings do. To know these things about yourself is a very sovereign quality.

And I believe there's a link to a Higher Power at work here too. I believe it's the connection between your Sovereign and your higher power, the force you recognize as greater than yourself, which provides the energy to propel your mission and sense of purpose in the world.

When you have a sense of your mission and purpose you're much more likely to embody sovereign energy. Apart from anything else, there's a quality about you that people recognize. It's a quality of presence and personal power which is implicit in the old saying "The world makes way for a man who knows where he is going."

What might your mission look like? Missions are very different from man to man and you can only know yours by seeking it out. When you do find it, you'll experience a settling in your body, a sense of the absolute rightness of what you're doing.

A friend of mine tells me his mission statement is "I bring people together with compassion and love in a spirit of unification and joy so that we can establish close connection and heal our wounds together." This is the mission by which he expresses his life purpose, which is "To create a family environment where everyone is welcome".

My own mission statement sounds like this: "I promote reconciliation between men, women and children, and between men and the planet, by facilitating healing circles in which people can bring their shadow into the light and so grow into emotional maturity." I see my soul purpose as empowering people to rediscover the truth of who they were always meant to be.

I don't know how many men in the world know their life purpose, or have a mission statement which supports it, but I do know that every Sovereign I respect is pretty sure of both of these things. Behind this, for me, lies a deeper question: are good Sovereigns made or are they born?

I think it's probably a combination of both, but what I know for sure is that each and every one of us has the potential to demonstrate sovereign energy in all or part of our lives and to step into it more consistently and more frequently than we presently do. And it can be a lot easier than you think.

Joy and Blessing

All true sovereignty involves leadership, and leadership can bring great joy. This idea is most clearly expressed in the concept of servant leadership coined by Robert K. Greenleaf in 1970. He said that a "servant leader" would start with a natural feeling of wanting to serve, and then he would make a conscious choice to do just that.

This is very different to most leadership in our society, which is driven by a desire for power or the acquisition of material goods or money. The essence of servant leadership is that the servant leader is primarily concerned with the well-being of other people.

The servant leader will always be a just and fair King (or Queen) whose highest priority is to make sure that those whom he is serving become healthier, better off, wiser and more evolved human beings because of his actions and leadership. What a joyous process, to see the fruits of your actions manifest in this way!

In short, a servant leader traditionally focuses on the growth and well-being of people and communities. His objective is personal growth and development for all. That is indeed true sovereignty at work, and joy is one of the rewards. (You can read more about this at Greenleaf.org)

Another important quality of the Sovereign, a quality which is shared with the true Elder, is that of blessing. Like sovereignty itself, we don't see much blessing in our society, but it's vitally important, especially for boys and young men, who crave the blessing and wisdom of their Elders. Yes, all children, both boys and girls, need affirmation and blessing from the energies of the masculine and feminine alike. But there is something truly exciting about the way a boy comes alive when he is blessed by his father or another older man. I believe boys have a need to be gifted a sense of their own Sovereign by being blessed by older men.

This raises, of course, the question of what blessing really means. Is it approval? Is it affirmation? Is it validation? I think it's simply an acceptance of the boy's right to exist just as he is without any conditions or expectations.

A friend of mine told me how one of his two boys was into sport, just like Dad. Father and son connected through soccer, going to watch professional team games together, and Dad coming along to watch his son playing in junior soccer games.

My friend's younger son was altogether different: more sensitive, less physical, much more studious, with a preference for connecting with his friends by quietly playing games at home with them. His father found this boring.

As time passed, the separation between them increased, until my friend took a step back and realized the damage he was doing to his younger son. He woke one morning, as he told me, with the clear sense that all he needed to do to put things right was to give his younger son his blessing. So, without forethought, he spontaneously stood in front of his son that afternoon, put his hand on the boy's shoulder, looked into his eyes, and said "Son, you're absolutely fine just the way you are." The boy melted into tears, hugged his father, and their relationship was restored from that day forward.

Which of us has not craved the blessing of our father?

And knowing how important that blessing would have been for you as a boy, take a moment to think how important your blessing may be, right now, to the citizens of your kingdom.

The blessing you offer your Queen may be a gesture of respect for her. Or some kind of honouring, perhaps simply time spent together.

The blessing you offer your children may be your time and presence, sharing some activities you enjoy (as well as the ones they enjoy but you do not), a loving gesture, a few words of approval or praise, a glance of understanding, or a way of showing your appreciation. Maybe it is a simple as saying "Good job, son." Only you can know what your blessing looks like.

For your employees or business associates, there will be another blessing, different again. So it goes, for as Sovereign one of your responsibilities is to see who needs blessing and to bless them freely, without expecting anything in return.

In Emotional Process Work and shadow healing workshops, we do an exercise where the men gather into groups of three, one playing the King and the other two acting as his subjects.

First the subjects invite the King to kneel before them so they can bless him, for a King can only rule with his subjects' agreement. They bless him without words by using their touch and their gaze, and by opening their hearts and sending him their own energy of blessing. After a couple of minutes they invite the King to rise, and they in turn kneel before him so he can give them his own blessing as King.

After everybody's had a turn in each role the energy in the room is extraordinary! It's shifted from separation and a lack of connection and trust, maybe even fear, to a palpable sense of connection, mutual appreciation, and shared equality and humanity. It's a most amazing exercise, and every time I watch it I see the extraordinary power of blessing once again.

Who will you bless in your life today?

Wisdom

The effort involved in holding your kingdom together when it's under pressure from all sides can be considerable. And so can the effort of holding your own emotional wounds at the same time as attending to the needs of family, business or friends. But that is the nature of Kingship – it's a 24/7 job, and you are never off duty.

How are you to survive, let alone thrive, in the face of such demands? By ensuring you have support, that's how.

Kings who prosper always draw on the wisdom of their counselors. These are advisers who support the King in the execution of his sovereignty and who make up for any deficit in the King's own experience or knowledge by finding and providing him with the advice and information he needs to rule wisely.

So it is with you, as King of your realm. You have the skill, knowledge and wisdom of your own internal Magician archetype available to you.

This is the part of you designed to provide answers to questions. In fact, it's the part of you which has been providing answers to questions since the day you were born. Your Magician's resources can lessen the burden for you as King and make it easier for you to rule with strength and certainty.

On another front, just as a King has support from his Warriors in holding the kingdom together, so you have your Warrior archetype ready to get things done in the world, ready to act as needed to hold the boundaries of your kingdom intact.

Your Warrior is the part of you responsible for going out into the world and getting things done, for finding ways to take action in the world which will support your mission and purpose as Sovereign.

As you see, the wisdom of your King includes knowing that you are not alone as you rule your kingdom. Another part of your wisdom lies in knowing how to use the resources of your Magician and Warrior. Let us also note that a good King fears not to draw on the wisdom and softness of his Lover archetype when he needs succour and support.

This might be as simple as enjoying the renewing touch of a massage or bodywork therapist, or it might be a deeper emotional process such as checking in with another circle of Sovereigns. But any King who tries to rule on his own, using nothing but his own power and wisdom, is ultimately destined to fail through lack of support.

So, to be a good King, to be a Sovereign who commands respect and continues to rule for his appointed time, you need to ensure that you have many mechanisms of support in place and that you are communicating freely with your own Warrior, Magician and Lover.

In our workshops we offer men the opportunity to step right into their Sovereign energy and experience the power they have inside themselves for real. When men do this, the way they see themselves starts to transform – and then they can begin to open up to the possibility of accepting a lot more leadership in their lives.

When you accept more leadership, you may find that you also take massive strides forward in forming a vision, knowing your purpose and having a sense of mission in the world.

And that can make your life feel worthwhile.

Resilience

Every good Sovereign will inevitably face challenges of one kind or another in life. As we all know, "Shit happens." Resilience is the key to surviving this: resilience is the ability to take the hits and keep bouncing back, as optimistic as ever.

Truth is, no matter how well prepared you might be to lead, no matter how much authority you might have, and no matter how much you might embody the qualities of the Sovereign, "Shit happens." What, then, can we do to develop our resilience in the face of everything the world can throw at us, whether expected or unexpected?

My view of resilience is that it emerges from inside you when you discover you can overcome adversity successfully by using your own resources. Does this mean that to be a Sovereign you must face adversity and overcome it? Possibly.

At the very least it means you must have enough resources to be able to respond to adversity with the conviction that everything will be alright, that you will survive, and that you will rebound from your wounds with a stronger self-esteem and more wisdom rather than a wounded heart full of resentment.

An Elder who I knew for a few years before he died, and who I respected greatly, drove his family mad by repeating the expression "strength through adversity" every time someone faced a problem. But I see the truth in this. I see it as a process akin to making steel, where forged steel is reheated in the crucible and emerges tempered into something much stronger. I believe we too can be forged into stronger material in the crucible of adversity simply because we learn what we are capable of, how strong we are.

Of course it's easy to say these things, and perhaps not quite so easy to live them! And those of you with little or no experience of sovereignty or leadership may well need some kind of training and support.

So at the end of this chapter I've offered some suggestions about how you might develop your sovereignty. But before we go there, let's look at the emotional wounding in this quarter and the shadows of the Sovereign which result from that wounding.

The Emotional Wound in the Sovereign Quarter

The emotional wound here is the wound of being told or shown that you are not good enough.

The average child is given thousands of opportunities to learn he's not good enough. The most obvious is constant criticism, either overtly or covertly. Overt criticism is obvious: "What did you do that for? Why did you do that? Can't you do it any better? If only you'd tried harder! You're useless…" You know the kind of thing, maybe.

Covert criticism comes in a million little pinpricks of insult, comments, poking fun, humiliations, and minor criticisms – or simply a lack of any praise – all of which diminishes rather than builds a child's self esteem. Regardless of how the message is delivered, the child senses its meaning – "You are simply not good enough." Or, more likely, "You are not good enough to be loved / to be accepted / to be liked / to be one of us." What might have been he message *you* received in your own family?

A caring parent who is wise enough to know how essential a strong sense of self-worth is in living a fulfilling life and achieving success will provide their son or daughter with plenty of positive support and encouragement. That's the kind of feedback which both supports his developing self-esteem and allows him room to grow and develop as a person in his own right.

Good feedback acknowledges and blesses a child's developing skills and knowledge. Such positive support encourages the growth of a child's Sovereign, but there is another essential element of support: giving a child clear boundaries. These promote an internal sense of safety and security.

A child who is blessed for what he does and who is provided with clear boundaries can internalize these positive messages. As he does so, he learns to manage his own life in a way that will serve him and, hopefully, allow him to serve the world.

When his parents gradually increase his responsibility, and support him as he begins to achieve more and more, he will learn how to express his power and authority in the world. As he does so, he gradually develops more and more sovereignty.

In essence, when a child experiences success he learns he is good enough and his sovereign energy grows. Sure, he may be unable to lead in all areas but he knows he can shine in many ways. And that in itself can be good enough.

However, when the opposite is true, and a child learns he is not good enough, perhaps not good enough to meet his parents' expectations, or those of his teachers, friends or family, the wounding can be profound. He internalizes failure, not success. His self-image becomes one of "I can't" rather than "I can". One of "I won't even try. I'll fail. I have nothing to offer."

Sadly for many children, the message they internalize is "I am nothing. I am worth nothing. I count for nothing."

I believe most people are wounded in this way to some degree, and most of us never recover from it. Yet because the wound and all that flows from it is held in the unconscious, where all our shadows are repressed and denied, you may not even know about it unless you set out to find it.

This is the Sovereign wound: anything which leaves you with a belief that you are not good enough to be the Sovereign in your own world. You may not feel it or know it, but it plays out, whether you are aware of it or not, in the way you present yourself in the world.

A belief that your achievements count for little or nothing. An unfelt sense of low self-worth which you act out all the time. You don't want to be seen; you don't deserve to be heard. You have nothing to offer, everywhere or in some particular areas of life. The specifics vary, the principle is the same: this is the wound of low-self worth, low self-confidence, low self-esteem.

The Sovereign wound seems to be the most widespread archetypal wound of all, for there are very few true Sovereigns in our world today. If you look around the current political, social, economic, environmental and business worlds you will be hard pressed to find many men and women who lead with power and dignity, with authority tempered by wisdom and discernment.

Instead, we see adolescent boy-men elected to political leadership, boy-men who are manifestly unsuited to govern, put in positions of assumed authority by those who project their own sovereign energy onto these no-hopers.

The Sovereign wound is a wound which shows itself in many ways. An obvious one is perfectionism. You see, perfectionism is simply a form of trying hard to be good enough. Unfortunately, when being good enough means being perfect, you're doomed to failure. Even if we were able to define what perfection means, how could anyone ever achieve it? Surely, it's impossible to be perfect? The truth is we can only ever be "good enough". And to appreciate that you are good enough is all that's required of a Sovereign. This means to be good enough for the task at hand. To be good enough for ruling your kingdom as it is.

But what, you may say, is good enough? In practice, good enough means knowing you can lead with authority, feeling confident as you do so. It's an internal sense of authority, knowing the rightness of your leadership, knowing you can lead (or if you prefer, since we are talking about the Sovereign here, "rule") with wisdom and good judgement; knowing, in fact, that you are up to the job in every way.

Another aspect of the Sovereign wound is a lack of resilience. We see this in someone who can't take the inevitable hits which life throws at him, someone who comes back weaker, not stronger, from these hits.

We all need resilience. There will always be people around us who are better or wiser than we are. There will always be people around us who simply want to take a pot shot at a Sovereign who's showing up. We will all inevitably face criticism and we will all inevitably make mistakes.

The mark of a strong Sovereign with a fundamentally strong sense of self-esteem and self-worth is that he will bounce back from these dips, knowing that he is indeed good enough to do the job and that he can continue to rule using all of his authority, wisdom and justice.

Someone without resilience, who can't take the hits and keep leading from the front, or someone who doesn't have the strength to lead from the front in the first place, is unlikely to feel good enough. And to the extent that a man does not feel good enough to be the Sovereign in his life, he will fail at what he's doing.

People with the most profound Sovereign wound are often children of parents who demanded more than they were ever able to provide.

On one workshop a woman immediately recognized her Sovereign wound when the facilitator spoke about the idea of "never being good enough". Her father, she observed, had always expected too much of her – more than she was capable of delivering.

When she arrived home from school with a test result of 98%, instead of praising her for this achievement, his inevitable reaction would be to criticize her by saying: "If you'd worked harder you could have achieved 100%." When the facilitator asked her what she thought might have satisfied her father, she paused for a moment and then said, "I think he'd have been satisfied if I'd become an astronaut." She wasn't joking. But the irony of her remark is that even then, he would not have been satisfied.

So this is the Sovereign wound: no-one ever told you that you were good enough just the way you were.

Sure, we all differ in our natural ability to cope with the demands that life makes of us. But given the right kind of encouragement, support and praise by our parents we all have the potential to develop a strong self-esteem and a powerful sense of self-worth. Sadly, a child's self-esteem is a delicate thing, and so his sovereign energy needs careful nurturing to grow and develop into its fullness and maturity. That's why all boys need a man they can look up to, a King who can offer them the consistent, clear, nurturing support of a father who understands what a Prince needs to develop naturally into a confident King.

When sovereign energy goes into shadow it can inflate into a false act of grandiosity or deflate into a sense of worthlessness. And as with the other archetypes, someone with a strong shadow Sovereign will switch between the inflated and the deflated polarities.

The Inflated Shadow: The Tyrant King

The word "tyrant" speaks of dominance, the misuse of power, and the outright abuse of authority. And a tyrant King does indeed misuse his power. Instead of seeing others as his subjects, to be treated with benevolence, the tyrant King sees everyone as a threat to his authority.

This vision of the world is a symptom of his narcissism. He believes he is the most important element of the universe and that everybody should serve him. Those who don't are a threat to his position, to his assumed authority and supremacy.

Underlying this viewpoint is a deep insecurity, an insecurity so profound that it causes him to lash out with physical, emotional or mental abuse at those whom he believes pose a threat to his authority and supremacy.

Only by putting others in their place can he maintain his own illusion of authority. But at same time, the tyrant King doesn't have any respect for others, merely seeing them as objects to exploit for his own ends. He will ruthlessly sacrifice people who might consider themselves to be under his protection, such as friends, family and employees, should he come to believe this is necessary to protect his own position. Another form of this is the man who achieves a position of power in the world of business or politics and then ruthlessly stabs in the back those who helped him reach that position.

Consumed with arrogance, with a sense of entitlement which is quite unjustified in any way, the tyrant continues to scream and shout his demands, expecting them to be fulfilled by the sycophants around him who are incapable of asserting their own boundaries or saying "No" to him. In childhood those people were his misguided parents. In adulthood, they are the unfortunate people who try to serve him.

Insecurity and low self-esteem bedevil the tyrant King. No matter what he achieves, it will never be enough to assuage the belief which eats away at the core of his being: the belief that he simply is not – and never will be – good enough. He may look powerful and confident, but it is all grandiosity, a falsehood, an act to cover up the deeply held feeling, the deeply held belief that he is not, and never can be, good enough.

Such men rarely show up on self-development workshops, or emotional healing workshops, because to do so is to admit the unthinkable – that they are in need of help. But sometimes men in this state do come along, pressured to do so by their wives. They generally leave quite quickly, disparaging the process and denying they could benefit in any way.

The Deflated Shadow:
The Weakling King, The Abdicating King

The passive, deflated shadow of the Sovereign archetype is the weakling King, the abdicating King. For some reason, a man may abdicate his throne. He hands over his sovereign power to others or allows others to take it from him. And along with power goes his responsibility, authority and control of his life. A common form of this is the man who, even as an adult, allows his mother, father, wife, or family to make all his decisions for him.

Maybe he never experienced power as a child, perhaps because he was raised by abusive or controlling parents. One way or another he was never given the chance to become responsible for his own well-being. And so, as an adult he may switch between the abdicating King, the passive or deflated shadow of the Sovereign, and the tyrant King, the active or inflated shadow, but in either case his insecurity always overcomes him.

He may become paranoid that people are out to get him – which they often are, because he's a fool and a jerk. He may become extremely controlling because he believes that's the only way to maintain his authority.

Moore and Gillette made the point that the tyrant and the weakling really work together. Every blustering tyrant hides a scared weakling, and every fearful weakling contains a tyrant waiting to explode.

If you experienced wounding in this archetype as a child, there's good news, however. No matter how severe your wounding may have been, there are ways in which you can develop your sovereign energy and generate the strength and confidence to lead in your own world. Here are some ideas about how you might achieve this.

The Golden Shadow

We tend to think of our shadow as a bad, dark thing, carrying the negative consequences of our emotional wounds. We saw above how the abdicating King and the tyrant King can indeed be the negative or dark shadows of the Sovereign archetype.

Yet there's another way to look at this: to consider the Golden qualities of the mature King, the King in his fullness, which we put into shadow. For we all put the positive aspects of ourselves which are not accepted by those around us into shadow just as adeptly as we stuff away the negative aspects of ourselves.

Who heard such statements as these during childhood? "Don't blow your own trumpet. Don't get too big for your boots. Pride goes before a fall. Don't get above yourself. They won't like you if you stand out." And so on… overtly or covertly, the message is clear: "Stay small." "Don't show your gold." "Don't think you are better than us."

And so your power, your confidence, your magnificence, your ability to lead, your integrity, your authenticity, your wisdom, your sense of justice, your capacity to strive for equality and fairness, your ability to bless others, your joy, your innate state of peace and balance, your vitality, your ability to hold the wounds of the kingdom, your ability to hold your own wounds, your acceptance of others as your equal, your celebration of humankind... all of these positive qualities, and many more, can form part of your unknown and unfelt Golden Shadow.

Collectively your Golden Shadow is made up of the positive aspects of your Sovereign archetype which you haven't expressed fully – or at all. Marianne Williamson wrote a powerful piece which you've probably heard or seen. It sums up the Golden Shadow.

"Our deepest fear is not that we are inadequate. Our deepest fear is that we are powerful beyond measure. It is our light, not our darkness that most frightens us. We ask ourselves, 'Who am I to be brilliant, gorgeous, talented, and fabulous?' Actually, who are you not to be? You are a child of God. Your playing small does not serve the world. There is nothing enlightened about shrinking so that other people will not feel insecure around you. We are all meant to shine, as children do."

Working on your Golden Shadows and releasing what they hold into your awareness is just as important to becoming who you were always meant to be as working on your Dark Shadows and accepting them as a part of who you are. So let's now take a look at some of the ways in which you can start to develop greater Sovereign energy and so reclaim your natural birthright as a human being: the expression of your true self, the man you were born to be.

How To Be A True Sovereign

1 Mix With Other Sovereigns

Men who are interested in achieving their full potential need to find a place where they can experience the power of their Sovereign archetype in a safe environment before taking it out into the world. Generally this means some kind of men's group or a workshop where you can work on your shadow.

The level of support and trust generated in these groups or workshops between the men who come with the desire to move into their power can be quite extraordinary. It's a real contrast to the competitive, dog-eat-dog way of behaving that some men display in the world at large.

There's another aspect to the workshop setting which is very important for encouraging sovereignty: men work together in an environment of trust and safety. This allows them to learn from each other, to discuss together what it means to be in Sovereign, and to get ideas about how they might take sovereign energy back into the reality of their lives.

And yes, theory has to be turned into reality in the world, but these groups act as a kind of reference point, home base, or solid anchor – use whichever metaphor you like – which show a man how he can be the Sovereign he wants to be in his life. For details of such workshops see the resources section of this book on page 179.

2 Find A Mentor

All powerful Sovereigns need a mentor. In fact, we all need a mentor. Why? Because we need support. We aren't designed to work it all out alone. Figuring out what it means to be a man can be hard enough. Figuring out what it means to be a King is even more of a challenge. Most men, I judge, don't have much in the way of supportive relationships with other men, let alone a mentor. So what's a mentor?

A man (or a woman) who is able to provide you with objective feedback, sound reflection, solid guidance and good advice. He'll tell you what you need to hear with compassion; he's a combination of coach, friend, therapist and wise Elder. He may be an expert in a particular field if that's what you need. In any event, he's a man who's got your back, come what may.

How do you find him? Start by looking around your world, and assess all possibilities. He may be waiting, in the form of a minister, counsellor, friend, Elder, coach… the possibilities are endless. A mentor doesn't have to be older than you, or exactly like you, or somebody whose achievements are obvious to all. A mentor is simply someone who can support you in the way you need to be supported. If you wish, you can have a particular man or woman who can serve you in this way in each of the various areas of your life.

3 Form A Sovereign Circle

As I approached the age of 60, my growing sovereignty called to me, and as it did so I became more aware of the challenge of living that sovereignty fully.

What has helped is my Sovereign circle. This is a group of men who come together to celebrate each others' achievements. The Sovereign circle is a development of the idea of the MasterMind group suggested by Napoleon Hill way back in 1925 in his book *"Think and Grow Rich"* – which is still in publication today.

Hill's idea was that men and women should get together in groups where they could support each other in the achievement of their financial goals. He believed that several people working together in harmony, in support of each other, could generate much more emotional, spiritual and physical energy than the sum of their individual efforts. In effect he was saying, "We're stronger together than separate." And so we are.

There's certainly a powerful force among a group of committed men working together in this way. This is a process which goes beyond our consciousness. In fact Napoleon Hill thought a MasterMind group could access the collective unconscious – call it universal intelligence, or cosmic consciousness, if you prefer. However, you don't need to believe in the concept of the collective unconscious to benefit from being part of a group of men who can support you.

I've been in several MasterMind groups over the years. The most recent one has naturally evolved into what we call our Sovereign Circle. This group is not just about offering practical support in business, valuable though that is. It's also about helping each other overcome our emotional blocks, providing positive support, and maintaining a judgement-free environment. It's a space where we can bring whatever we need to bring, safe in the knowledge that we will not be judged or criticized. Rather, we will be supported in what we want to achieve in our lives.

If you want to know more you can easily research the idea of a MasterMind group on the Internet. Read all about it, and then form your own group in the way that best suits your objectives.

An important element of the MasterMind group or Sovereign Circle is that you form it with people who are at or above your own level of development. That way, you will be stretched. After all, you won't become a stronger Sovereign by staying inside your existing comfort zone!

4 Develop Your Leadership

Since sovereign energy is so much about leadership, you might like to seek out some self-development workshops which aim to develop the quality of leadership. For you, this might mean an Outward Bound course or a Survival Skills course. It may mean attending a workshop run by experts in the human archetypes. It might mean going through a weekend of self-development experiences like those offered by the ManKind Project. It may mean finding a training course to develop your leadership skills in business, perhaps in your particular area of expertise. It may mean finding a coach to support you in your personal or business life.

The simple fact is, you don't have to do it all alone, and like any Sovereign, you need support as you develop the skills necessary for the expression of your Kingship.

5 Explore Your Purpose and Mission – Form A Vision

If you don't know what you want for your kingdom, if you have no vision for the future of yourself and your citizens, you are not fully in your sovereignty.

After all, you cannot lead your people to a better future when you have no vision for them! And because you are your own Sovereign, you need to answer these questions for yourself: what is your purpose on this Earth? What is your vision for your kingdom? What is your mission in life? How do your vision and mission relate to your soul purpose?

To make this clearer, you might try thinking of your soul purpose as what you could achieve by your very presence on planet Earth; the thing you were put here to do, as it were. You can think of your vision as what your Kingdom would look like as you strive to fulfil your purpose, and you can think of your mission as how you manifest your purpose. In other words, your mission might reflect the practical path you can take to achieve a higher purpose.

For example, a friend of mine is a yoga teacher. He tells me his soul purpose is to help men and women grow into who they truly are. His mission is to bring the gifts of self-knowledge and awareness to men and women by teaching yoga. His vision includes a well-being centre where yoga workshops and healing can take place.

When you have answered those questions, a vital step is for you as your own Sovereign to set yourself goals and objectives. These are achievable steps along the path to achieving your vision.

Goals make your Warrior sit up and take notice. He waits for his orders from you, your instructions about how he can go out into the world and make your goals and objectives become a reality.

If the ideas of soul purpose, vision and mission sound like a mystery, fear not! There are many websites, workshops and people who can help you to establish what all this might mean for you. Use the energy of your Magician to seek these resources out, and apply the discernment and wisdom of your Sovereign to decide which path is right for you.

A Sovereign needs to have a clear vision for his kingdom, and a sense of his own life purpose and mission at every stage of his life. These evolve as time goes by. Happily these days, we have the Internet available to us as a repository of just about all the information we could ever need to understand such matters.

One final point: understanding your purpose and having a mission in the world is an important first step, but what really counts is taking action. That is the value of setting goals and objectives: they motivate your Warrior to take action.

6 Develop Practical Wisdom or Common Sense

There's a big difference between the theoretical knowledge of a clever Magician and the application of the practical wisdom we all need to live successfully in the world. We call this practical wisdom "commonsense", but why some people have it and some don't is a bit of a mystery.

We can define "commonsense" as the practical application of knowledge in a way that meets both your own needs and the needs of the people around you. John Bradshaw describes it as "the ability to do the right thing, at the right time, for the right reason".

Of course developing such practical wisdom is partly down to experience. The more decisions you make, and the wiser they are, the better your outcomes and the more positive and affirming your feedback.

You can see how this ties in with the concept of resilience: you discover you can cope with whatever the world throws at you, then you learn how to deal with it appropriately, you come back for more, and you find this time you can do it better. In short, you consistently improve in everything you do, all the time.

The more you seek out life experiences that challenge you and allow you to develop your skills, the more likely you are to develop the practical wisdom that will support your sovereignty.

7 Get Your Balls Back From Anyone Who Has Them

If you find yourself reverting to a childhood pattern of thoughts, feelings and behaviour in the presence of your parents, particularly in the presence of your mother (or in the presence of any other woman, for that matter), then your Sovereign energy may need to be strengthened.

As a child, you may have had good reason to please your mother – usually to stay safe in some way. You may have come to believe you were controlled by your mother. You may have grown to fear feminine anger, or been shamed by the feminine, as represented by your mother. These and many more distortions of relationship are all common enough in men.

But here's the thing: adult men tend to relate to women on the basis of their childhood experience of Mother. (And yes, we also learn how to relate to men by extrapolating our relationship with Father. But true emancipation of the male soul and true growth into sovereignty is achieved by liberation from the control of the feminine.)

For as long as you remain under the control of the feminine, you will carry some degree of self-hatred. That's because at some level, conscious or unconscious, you know you're being controlled. You know you haven't achieved the emotional freedom needed to be a man in your own right. You know you're not free, as a Sovereign in your kingdom, to make the choices you want to make. You're constrained by another, maybe by mother. Someone else has got your balls.

It isn't in the natural order of things for a man to be controlled by the feminine (or vice versa). Indeed, to fully develop as a mature man you have to break away from the feminine, as represented by Mother, sometime in your boyhood, your adolescence, or even your adult life. (It's never too late!) Only then can you begin to identify fully with your masculine essence.

None of this means that your relationship with the feminine comes to an end or, let us hope, morphs into a relationship based on domination of the feminine by you. It simply means that before you can become a man fully in your own power, you have to break away from the control of the feminine – as represented, most likely, by Mother.

Men who have not broken free in this way tend to give away their power to women. They feel bad about the fact that they can't stand up to women and maintain their boundaries. They carry some self-hatred about this pattern.

And this dynamic is what makes men lie to women: a man who feels he is too weak to stand up to a woman may also believe he must appease her lest she get angry. His objective is to avoid conflict even under intolerable pressure, simply because he doesn't have the masculine strength to keep his boundaries and his masculine identity intact in the face of a woman's assault on them.

It's a humiliating situation for a man to be in: he knows he is weak, that he is a mommy's boy at heart. And his woman knows it, too. Nor is she about to let him forget it. She may push him all the time until he shows some balls. Unfortunately he hasn't got any, so rather than displaying them in the form of a clear boundary, he's most likely to explode in rage or skulk off, neither of which does his self-esteem much good.

If you have any reason to think that your mother still believes she controls you, or she behaves as if she does, or if you respond to her in ways which suggest this could be true, then you need to get a grip on your masculinity. (And the same is true, of course, if your father took away your masculinity or denied you the right to step into your power.)

One possibility here is to develop a mature relationship with the feminine – firstly with your mother, if that's possible, though it is often not, and secondly with women in general. This can be a respectful and loving relationship, even considerate and helpful, but it should never leave you in a position of weakness and subjugation to the childhood dynamics of your relationship with mommy.

What does this mean in practice? Many things. For example, you must put the needs of your family before the needs of your mother. If she becomes critical of you and what you do, stop talking to her and leave. When she visits, you and your woman agree the terms of those visits beforehand. She takes care of your children only with your consent and only in a way with which you agree. And so on. If you wish to be a man who's reclaimed his balls, then you have to make a stand.

However, while these ideas may seem attractive, it's not always so easy to put them into practice, and you may well need support in this area. That might look like a circle of men who can support you, hold you accountable, and encourage you to see this through. Or you could join a men's workshop and find out how to get your balls back.

By the way, this is not about blaming your mother (or father) for what she did. Rather, it's about accepting her for the person she is, and seeing her as someone from whom you now need nothing and on whom you are not dependent.

In short, this is about becoming a man who can stand in his own power.

8 Do What You Want To Do & Be True To Yourself

How easily influenced are you by the opinions of others? How often do you give up your own interests and ambitions because of the judgements and criticism of other people?

To put it more bluntly, are you able to pursue your own heart's desires in the face of judgements, criticism, or even ridicule from other people? How do you respond to this? And how much do you stop yourself enjoying the things which excite you and make you happy, the things you really want, because of what others might say or think?

To be truly free in this way, you might need the support of some good male buddies, a place to vent your anger, and some training in assertiveness which will allow you to speak your mind in a safe way. This will help you develop the male energy needed to become better able to resist the expectations and demands of others. A supportive men's group is an important element of this process, too. If you don't have access to a men's group, you could always start one. It's not hard: the suggested reading list towards the end of this book includes a classic book which tells you how to do it. And you will find growing into your Sovereign is much easier when you have male support of this kind.

You may also find that as your sovereign energy grows and becomes more obvious and more clearly seen, people around you may start to offer unhelpful criticism and judgements. They may try to draw you back into your old ways of being so they feel safe. You need to keep a close watch on how you are faring in the world so you can be sure you're following your true path rather than being led astray by others with their own agenda. This is where having a mentor, a wise counselor, and a men's group made up of men you trust to support you and offer honest feedback is essential.

As Sovereign you need to be confident of following your own inner compass rather than allowing yourself to be guided by the trashy voices of a thousand different media channels bombarding you with propaganda every day. That includes emails, texts, Facebook, Twitter and the like. If avoiding them seems impossible, try a digital detox. Look it up on Google if needed. Then give up the tech.

We men also need a space in which we can spend time alone with ourselves so we can better understand our own inner world. I recommend time spent in Nature as a part of this process, perhaps one day a month in a place where you feel at ease and able to connect with something bigger than yourself: Mother Nature, Planet Earth.

At heart, everything you're doing here is forming a male identity which is truly your own and fits you exactly in thought, word and deed. Once you have a clear sense of who you are and what you stand for, you will be much less influenced by the opinions, beliefs and judgements of other people, and immune to the time-wasting nonsense that flows over you from those trashy media channels.

9 Develop Integrity & Know What You Stand For

Integrity is one of the most profound human values – and, I believe, one of the most difficult to embody and live with on a day-to-day basis. But what do we mean by integrity?

To put it simply, you have integrity when you are who you say you are, you do what you say you will do, and you make yourself responsible for the consequences of your actions, both intended and unintended.

Beyond these simple maxims, integrity means having a set of principles by which you live, and knowing precisely what those principles are. Some men refer to them as NUTS – short for "nonnegotiable, unalterable terms". This is a neat way of reminding ourselves that our balls are a major part of what make us men.

Your NUTS are what help you become a man of integrity; they are the things to which you are committed, without question. As a man, you need to find your NUTS and keep a firm grasp of them.

Your NUTS might be centered on your kids, your relationships, your purpose, your spiritual practice, your boundaries, your morals – anything, in fact.

These are the things that define YOU as a man. You keep them sacred, you aspire to protect them. They are the things which you will defend whole-heartedly. If you allow others to compromise these values, with or without your permission or acquiescence, you may find yourself becoming resentful and blaming.

For example, your NUTS might be summed up in a series of short statements like this:

I am a risk taker.
I am faithful to my wife or partner.
I devote at least three hours a week to my spiritual practice.
I do not allow people to infringe my boundaries under any circumstances.
I am honest.
I support my children in the face of any threats to their well-being.
I do what I believe to be in the best interests of my children even if they disagree with me.
I do not indulge my addictions.
I never use porn.
I never abuse women in thought, word or deed.
I stand up for those less well-off than myself.
I am a man of my word.
I exercise regularly.
I never apologize simply to placate or please others.
I decide how to interact with my children.
I only maintain friendships which serve me.

And so on. You can see how this works, I'm sure. Find your first thirty NUTS right now, and write them down. Pin them up somewhere so you can see them every morning. Reflect on your NUTS regularly, so that you know what you stand for and you know where your boundaries lie. This process can show you the core values which lie at the very centre of who you are and how you present yourself in the world.

The essence of integrity is knowing what you stand for. It's rare to see such clear sovereignty in young men, because they are at a developmental stage where they are often driven by a need to go out into the world and make their mark. But occasionally I come across young men who are clearly Princes: Kings in waiting. Tom, a young man of 23 who I was counselling recently, came up with some truly profound values when we talked about integrity and what he wanted to stand up for:

Equality of people.
Justice for all.
Freedom of expression
Supporting the power of the common man.
Defending the rights of the oppressed.
Supporting the right to be truly yourself.

You could spend a few minutes now thinking about your own values, the values that underlie your NUTS. Simply start by jotting down all the ideas which come to mind – you can always refine them later. The important thing here, I believe, is to start thinking about what really matters to you. And reflecting on the qualities you admire in others is often helpful in identifying the qualities you would like to embody yourself.

10 Act With Intention

One of the most powerful aspects of sovereignty is forming an intention and acting upon it. For example, in the list above you will see this statement: "I do not indulge my addictions." Addictions serve as a great way to illustrate the power of intention.

Over the years I have heard many, many men declare that they will give up porn, drugs, drink, gossip, sweet food and all the other addictions which seem to soothe some deeply wounded part of us all, only to find that after a week or a month or a year they drift back into the same old pattern. Why is this?

There seem to be two main reasons.

First, they have not set a clear intention for change. They have not thought about what it would really mean for this change to be a part of who they are, nor whether it fits with what they truly want at this time in their lives.

To consciously set an intention for yourself requires a clear choice about what you want, born of a clear decision about what is best for you at this time in your life – for example, giving up alcohol or drugs. Setting a clear intention about *what you want* means you stand much less chance of being swayed or distracted by the prevailing opinions of the people around you (who may wish to maintain the status quo).

Also, setting an intention means you have great clarity about what you're trying to achieve, and that clarity allows you to hold yourself accountable if you fail to move in the right direction. If you have an accountability buddy, so much the better. That's a buddy who can check in with you on a regular basis to see how you're doing with your intention, and who is willing to really listen as you speak about what's going on for you.

The second reason is more challenging. You may not be in a place of sufficient internal strength to give up your addictions. And this brings us to the essential element of how to deal with your emotional wounds so you can become the Sovereign you want to be.

We all carry a wounded little boy inside of us; he's a part of who we are. So, for example, if your wounded inner child is demanding to be soothed with alcohol or drugs or food or sex, and his demands are stronger than your conscious intention not to indulge in those things, I'm sure you already know how this will turn out.

(In case you're wondering, your inner child will most likely prevail. And you'll be back to the PC watching porn, getting the whisky bottle out, eating trashy food, smoking dope, or whatever…)

To beat yourself up about this is pointless. The right course of action is to find a way of working with your inner child to soothe him.

Most wounded inner children lacked good parenting, and this is what they still need. So you could be a father to him; to put it another way, you could be his Sovereign. You can father your inner child by talking to him, holding him, and indulging him in a good-father kind of way, just as you would for your own son or daughter. You can also set a loving boundary around his actions, just as you would if he was your own physical child. This way he will come to feel more safe and more loved, and the intensity of his pain will diminish.

Another benefit of attending to the needs of this part of yourself is that his urge to hijack your entire system will become much less compelling, which means your Sovereign can take his rightful place as leader in your kingdom without fighting the powerful demands of an unhappy little boy.

11 Be Decisive

Sure, this isn't always easy. But decisiveness is a clear trait of all powerful Sovereigns. Decisiveness engenders respect from men and women alike. Sometimes making a decision and sticking to it can be more helpful than questioning yourself and changing your mind numerous times. That can be a sign of weakness and may diminish your chance of achieving success in the longer term.

Developing the quality of decisiveness allows you to be calm and cool under pressure, to be the person who keeps his head when all about are losing theirs (and perhaps blaming it on you).

Decisiveness also allows you to be self-motivating when times are hard or circumstances challenging. It allows you to stay calm more easily under pressure, perhaps when the children are provoking you beyond reason, your employees are making demands on you that seem unreasonable in the extreme, and you're battling all kinds of pressures in your relationship too.

You will stay calm because you know what to do in a crisis, and you are confident about doing it. You are, after all, a Sovereign who can hold the wounds of his kingdom, because you've developed the skills and strengths that allow you to do this.

There are other advantages to being decisive, too.

Decisiveness of this kind allows you to move swiftly towards your goals and to move towards happiness and fulfilment quickly and easily. You're in control of yourself and the world around you. You know what you want and you know where you're going. You are, in fact, the master of your own destiny.

Making informed and good decisions is easier with the assistance of your Magician. You can ask him to get all the information you need before you make a decision. Let him be creative and imaginative about getting it, and ensure that you assess the information he offers to you carefully. As far as may be possible, imagine the consequences of each choice you could make. Cross-reference all this with your past experience, and then decide what to do. Learn to trust your intuition.

The more you face up to challenges, the more you'll be able to cope with any situation that arises, no matter how unexpected. When you do this, your confidence and self-assuredness will grow quickly.

A few words of practical wisdom: avoid regret about the decisions you've already made. The constructive thing here is to learn from your mistakes and move forward knowing how to do things differently in the future. Energy spent on worrying is energy wasted; energy expended on your regrets keeps you trapped in the past, and is not available to propel you towards your future.

Strengthening your sovereignty in all these ways will allow you to accept the mistakes you've made, forgive yourself, and move on – and even if you do have regrets, you will be able to hold them with a sense of self-compassion and love.

The Boyhood Sovereign Archetype – The Divine Child

Boys have all the archetypes of the mature masculine within them in an "immature" form – in other words, in a form that prefigures the same archetype in the mature masculine.

Moore and Gillette called the boyhood form of the Sovereign archetype the Divine Child. If you've ever held a newborn baby boy or girl, you may have felt this energy of the Divine Child in its most pure and innocent form. Working on your shadows and healing your emotional wounds will allow you to reconnect with this childhood energy to some degree, and as you do that, you will move closer to recovering your true nature.

Perhaps the Divine Child is a state of being, an energy that is hardwired into our brains when we are born: an energy that gives us a natural sense of our capacity to do anything we want as well as an awareness of our glorious magnificence and, yes, perhaps even our divinity.

Sadly, the world may not take very kindly to this sort of energy in the child. Heinz Kohut, a pioneer in the field of self-psychology, referred to it as "grandiose self-organization" which demands of ourselves and others what can never be provided or fulfilled.

The Jungian perspective, however, shows us how this archetypal energy is the source of our life force. It empowers us, produces an enormous sense of confidence, self-esteem and well-being, and it fosters our enthusiasm for life. This is the energy that keeps us young at heart and propels us happily, with a sense of the rightness of the way things are, all the way through our lives, even into death.

The Shadows of the Divine Child

The inflated pole of the Divine Child is the high chair tyrant. This is a truly immature form of sovereign energy, summed up in the image of a little boy having a tantrum because his demands are not being met while simultaneously demanding that the world should immediately respond to his needs and do as he requires.

The problem is, anything that isn't quite right is rejected with anger. The high chair tyrant experiences – and expresses – limitless demands, a symptom of his own grandiosity, but regrettably because he believes his needs can never be met, he turns away from what is offered, even the love that he needs to nurture him.

Arrogance and childishness and irresponsibility are the hallmarks of this shadow. The problem is that the high chair tyrant has somehow come to believe that he is the centre of everyone's universe, and that everyone and everything has been provided to meet his every need. This tyranny is an infantile state of mind: that of the indulged and pampered infant who grows into a boy who's equally mollycoddled, a boy who then becomes a man with no sense of responsibility or obligation to the world around him

For a man who continues to carry the high chair tyrant into adulthood, progress in the world may, for a while at least, be rapid – there have always been plenty of people in the world willing to serve a tyrant. Yet these men are so-called leaders who can't tolerate an opposing viewpoint or take criticism or challenge, and who throw a tantrum when things don't go their way. Possessed by the energy of the high chair tyrant, they may get rid of anyone who opposes them; even so they don't usually survive for very long.

The unfortunate problem for anyone possessed by this archetype is that the demands of the high chair tyrant can never be met. The grandiose two-year-old inside the man, the grandiose five-year-old inside the man, the grandiose teenager inside the man – these are the energies which drive the apparently adult man to ever more outrageous behaviour.

As Moore and Gillette put it, unless the high chair tyrant is brought under control, he will finally manifest as a modern version of Stalin, Caligula, or Hitler. There are plenty of modern day examples, too.

No matter that the grandiosity and sense of entitlement of people like Hitler ends in the destruction of their own country – all that matters to them is their own grandiosity, and getting their own needs met. Which is, of course, impossible.

The deflated shadow of the divine child is the weakling Prince. This is an energy of passivity, withdrawal, weakness, and helplessness. Yet this is a front for something more malicious: a more manipulative, vicious, almost predatorial energy which is pretending to be a helpless victim.

Although this is a most unpleasant energy to be around, in its way as unpleasant as the high chair tyrant, it's still an energy that occupies a throne, for this aura of victimhood tends to draw protective energy from others with a certain complementary need (his parents, first and foremost).

As with all shadows, a victim child in the deflated form of the archetype can switch into the opposite pole and – in this case – start to display tyrannical outbursts.

Although these shadows are dysfunctional, the Divine Child in its balanced form is a powerful archetype for a boy to inhabit. And it's a powerful archetype when it lives on within the grown man, too.

The skill here is achieving maturity: inhabiting the mature Sovereign archetype while recognizing the value of the immature Divine Child within. It's important for a mature man not to identify with the Divine Child, but to simply connect with it and its energy: the energy of creativity, vitality, greatness, perhaps even some kind of connection to our innate perfection.

We need to watch for the Divine Child's shadows throughout our lives. As Moore and Gillette put it, the question is not *whether* we are manifesting the high chair tyrant or the weakling Prince, but *how* we are manifesting them. As they said, at the very least we're all manifesting them when we regress into our inner child when we're frightened or tired!

And still, we need to honour this inner child, the Divine Child within, for his positive qualities; they are life-giving. If we're not feeling his energy, the right response might be to consider how we're blocking him – and why we're doing so.

In Summary

The Sovereign archetype is what the world needs more than anything right now. It encompasses – in its balanced form – a care for the Earth, the people, the environment and the self. It reflects generosity of spirit, and carries an understanding that we are all derived from the same energy source. This allows the Sovereign to acknowledge that we are more similar than different, an insight which is the foundation of an attitude of respect to all the citizens of the world.

At the same time, the King will rule without fear or favour, knowing that his responsibility extends to the seventh generation, and that he is only a temporary custodian of what is in his care today.

As a man who knows he is good enough, he can be generous to others and their failings, and so he responds to their projections gracefully.

He lives from a place of humility, for he respects the natural order of things, and he does not take his sovereignty for granted.

He feels joy because he embodies emotional maturity. He has done much of his personal work and is able to bless others with a generous and open heart, respecting them as the unique manifestation of the divine that they are.

He knows with visceral certainty the inevitability of his own death. He grasps this as a physical reality, not just as a theoretical idea, and this knowledge softens his drive and ambition. "This too shall pass" means rather more to him than the average person.

He may embody the qualities of an Elder, recognizing the need to support younger men on their Hero's journey. He will look back on his life from his death bed with a sense of satisfaction, knowing that he has done what he can, and that he was indeed good enough.

Chapter 6

Your Shadow Uncovered: Exploring Your Unknown Inner World

Shadow: the parts of yourself which you hide, repress and deny. Sounds simple, doesn't it? But is it? For one thing, how would you know which parts of yourself you've put into shadow? And what does this really mean, anyway?

Robert Bly summarized the concept of shadow very simply. He wrote about young children having a "360 degree personality". They are complete, whole. The energy of life energy radiates out from young children, from both body and psyche.

A child running, says Bly, is "a rounded, living globe of energy". And it's certainly true: when you look at children you can see their energy so clearly. Sadly, you can also see how parents quickly convey to a child that certain parts of his or her rounded globe of energy are less welcome than others.

They ask a child, "Can't you just be quiet?" "Can't you sit still for a minute?" "Why can't you be more like your big brother?" "Why can't you just be a good boy for a change?" Such comments convey a message infused with disapproval, rejection or disappointment, and each message changes how the child behaves, thinks or feels about himself. Sometimes the messages are very direct; they may take the form of physical, emotional or sexual abuse which really conveys the message to a child that he is bad, worthless, has no power, is unloved, or something else hugely damaging.

Parents also send messages about what is expected of a child when they say things like, "Big boys don't cry." (Which really means, don't be vulnerable or show your sadness.) "You should stand up for yourself more." (You're weak, and we're not going to help you.) "You want to be good at sports, don't you?" (Your talents, wishes and choices are not valid in our minds.) "Boys should be strong and brave." (Your fear is not welcome here.) Some messages are cleaner, healthier and more useful than others: "It isn't nice to hit your brother." "Don't tease the cat." "Be polite and share with the other boys and girls."

While children fare better in life if they are socialized, for example by being taught not to hurt their most unwelcome new baby brother or sister, parents may go well beyond this. For reasons of their own, they may try to suppress certain natural energies in their child's personality – his tears, maybe, or his anger, fear, self-confidence, joy, creativity, wildness, exuberance, spontaneity, curiosity and sexuality.

Each of these is an energy which a child can put away, out of sight, if his parents don't want it, don't like it, or won't tolerate it. And where does it all go? Into the shadow bag, a highly expandable imaginary bag conveniently slung over our shoulder and into which we can put everything our parents, friends, siblings, teachers, and society don't like or want in us.

As children, we put things into this bag because we want our parents to love us in the moment and to continue loving us into the future. As children, it seems that stuffing parts of ourselves out of sight, into what we call the shadow, is an obvious and easy way to become what others want us to be.

To be more specific, your shadow is made up of your unwanted childhood characteristics (unwanted either by you or by others), and your shadow bag is in fact your unconscious.

And so we put into our shadow bags the parts of ourselves which don't meet with our parents' approval. But even then we are not safe. Siblings and peers exert pressure to conform. Our society and culture has many expectations of what boys and girls should put into their shadow bags. Girls may put away their anger so it's out of sight. To be angry may not be lady-like. Boys may put away their tears. After all, it's not manly for a boy to cry, is it?

Early childhood is only the start of this process, however. When we move on to junior or elementary school, high school and even university, we stuff more and more parts of ourselves into our shadow bag. That's because peer approval is an extremely important part of our social world – no matter what age we may be.

A shadow bag slung over your shoulder is a perfect metaphor for several qualities of your shadow. First, this imaginary bag lies over your shoulder, behind you, and this reminds you that your shadow, which carries all the repressed parts of you, is out of sight.

Second, just like a real bag which you have to carry around, the shadow bag over your shoulder can be very heavy, and can drain a great deal of energy from you. Yet it's not so much carrying the bag that drains your energy as the effort required to keep the things you've stuffed into the bag, inside the bag. Strangely, no matter how hard you try to keep them in there, they're always going to leak out anyway – often at the most inappropriate moment, as you probably already know.

And third, if you stuff a large proportion of your emotions and behaviour into your shadow bag, you're obviously stuffing a large proportion of your personality into that bag, out of sight. And by the time you're an adult – say 21 years of age – you may be left with only a small fraction of the complete 360 degree personality, the rounded ball of energy, you were born with.

Fourth, like your sun-lit shadow, you can't get rid of it. It's always with you. Sometimes you see it, sometimes you don't. But it's yours for life. Unless, that is, you take the infinitely courageous step of opening the bag and taking the contents out and reacquainting yourself with the parts of your personality you stuffed away long ago. Why do that, you might ask? After all, those parts of you went in the bag for a good reason.

Well, yes, that is true. Or, more exactly, it was true when you were growing up. And yet they can come out for an equally good reason: so you can become more of who you were always meant to be, before the world got in the way.

When you take the repressed parts of yourself out of shadow you begin to change: to grow, to mature. In fact this is one of the best ways of working on your personal growth and development. (People have a variety of names for this work: archetypal coaching, archetypal counselling, Emotional Process Work, emotional healing, healing the shadow, or simply Shadow Work.)

As you do this work, you'll find you're much less likely to be emotionally "triggered" by others. The more work on your shadow you do, the less triggered you'll be. You'll regain your natural personality. You'll get much more conscious control over your thoughts, feelings and actions.

Above all, you can take back control of your life and stand in your power and potency, knowing what's true for you, knowing that you have a right to exist just the way you are, a right to occupy the space you stand in, and a right to consciously choose who and what you are in the world.

Sadly, most people seem to keep their shadow bag slung over their shoulders, dragging it around for the rest of their lives. Thing is, though, the energy of what's repressed into shadow doesn't go away. In fact it actually grows because it hasn't got anywhere much to go. But whenever a slight opening appears in the top of the bag, the energy of your shadow emerges. What emerges can be powerful and frightening, twisted and warped, even monstrous; certainly it can look very different to the way it did when it went into the bag all those years before.

Another possibility: sooner or later the weight of the bag becomes so heavy that you decide something has to be done. It's wearing you out. Life isn't going the way you want. You struggle. You know life should be easier than this. You can't seem to change things. Your relationships fail. You're addicted. You can't keep boundaries. So you open the bag, peer inside, and embark on what can be (if you so choose) a lifelong process of pulling things out of the bag, claiming them as your own, and reintegrating them into your personality.

Just one thing, though. When you pull things out of the bag, they don't look quite like they did when they went in. They seem different. In Robert Bly's words, they have "de-evolved towards barbarism", and that's really why they need to come out. I believe they don't so much "de-evolve" as gradually build up more and more energy which can transform them into an all-too-powerful shadow version of themselves.

Among other things, children may bag up their anger, fear, grief, their natural sexuality, their wildness, their impulsive nature, their spontaneity, their creativity, their appreciation of themselves, and their sense of self-worth. For good measure, most boys also bag up their feminine side – the Anima, as Carl Jung called it – to a greater or lesser degree. That's what we expect in our culture: most men want "manly" or "masculine" sons. And with such an enormous but unspoken set of expectations contributing to his internalized image of masculinity, what else is a boy to do but go along with it?

Anyhow, life goes on, at least for a while, with greater or lesser ease. It takes a lot of energy to hold all these things in the bag and so they leak out now and again, often unhelpfully, but even so life looks more-or-less OK. At least the owner of the bag can survive with it.

Heavy though his bag is, the energy of the man's Hero archetype helps to keep him going.

Sooner or later though, things change. The bag's being topped up all the time. It gets heavier. Even Heroes get tired. And if a man hasn't opened his shadow bag by the time he's forty or fifty – and sometimes much sooner – the energy inside will be ready to find its own way out, disrupting his life, causing problems, perhaps even creating misery.

Much better, then, that a man finds a place where he can open his shadow bag with support. A safe enough space, like an Emotional Process Workshop run by facilitators skilled in the arts of emotional healing. Why a workshop? Well, when a man decides to open the bag because something just isn't right in his life, there may be trouble ahead. Simply, it's better to be supported when you open your bag!

A man can't have good sexual relationships, maybe, so he opens the bag and finds a hurt child inside who's raging at woman. Maybe he explodes with anger at the least provocation, so he opens the bag and finds a very angry and hurt little boy raging at him. Perhaps he feels meek and mild, like a man without boundaries, so he opens the bag, only to find a victimizing bully who wants to destroy everything around him.

Or perhaps he can't run his own life or accept the responsibility of leadership, so he opens the bag, only to find a raging tyrant or an abdicating King living inside. He already knows, most likely, about the addict in the bag without even looking inside. That one really frightens him because he seems to have no control over it at all!

And finally, when his relationships with women break down, he may open the bag, only to find his own feminine energy and the sexual desires he put in there have taken on a very different appearance: they've become hostile to him. Robert Bly believed that when we put our shadow into the bag, it becomes hostile to us, and is then reflected back at us in life. His principle was: the outside becomes like the inside.

Not all shadow is negative. Often it contains a great deal of "gold" – positive qualities which weren't acceptable to others when we were children. This might include qualities like vulnerability, tenderness, compassion, empathy, love, assertiveness, confidence, magnificence, power and potency. Maybe you have a sense of your own "missing" golden qualities, the ones you put into shadow as a child.

These positive qualities go into the bag because in many cultures children are taught that it's wrong to be "too big for your boots", that "pride goes before a fall", that it's wrong to "blow your own trumpet", and so on. So where do they put their self-confidence, self-worth and self-esteem? Into shadow.

Children do this to conform to the expectations of the people and culture around them. The logic seems simple to a child: "If I conform, I will be accepted. If I do not, I will be rejected." Given this situation, most children will choose acceptance every time. Fortunate indeed are those whose differences and special qualities are nurtured and encouraged.

(The film *Billy Elliot*, based on a true story about a boy from a coal mining town in England who wanted to become a ballet dancer – and managed to do so – reminds us that a few children somehow find the energy to defy the norms of family or culture and still thrive.)

The reality is that children can be humiliated and diminished, whether unconsciously or deliberately, by many things. They may suffer hurts to their self-esteem at the hands of parents, relatives, other adults, siblings, teachers, and the school system. They may be shamed because they do not have the "right" talents, appearance, or abilities for the culture in which they live. They may want to do things which do not meet the expectations of the people around them, who then choose to see them as different, weird, or perhaps even abnormal – and reject them.

We all know it can be hard to feel different. Which of us, as a child, did not want to be popular, good or "normal" in the eyes of those around us? Which of us did not want to be accepted by the others?

This desire for acceptance explains why so many children gradually hide more and more of themselves. But, as we've seen, what goes into your shadow bag, whether positive or negative, will change in character.

Anger may become rage, sadness can build into deep grief which burdens a man's soul. Repressed sexuality may transform into an addiction to sexual kinks, or the victimization of women. Fear may become acute and irrational anxiety, devoid of connection with reality. Self-protection and risk management can transform into judgementalism, cynicism or predatorial behaviour.

As for a boy's sense of self-worth and self-importance, well, when shoved into shadow, they may inflate into grandiosity or collapse into a sense of insignificance. When you see someone who has a grossly inflated sense of his own superiority and grandiosity, it's a fair assumption that most of his self-worth and self-esteem were beaten (maybe literally, maybe metaphorically) out of him as a child.

The same is true when you see a man who's playing small, hiding his abilities and not daring to show the world who he really is. As a boy, he probably put most if not all of his self-worth into his shadow bag. This somehow kept him safe from shame and humiliation, or worse.

Alice Miller, one of the pioneering child psychotherapists of the twentieth century, wrote a book called *The Drama Of The Gifted Child*. In that book she described the drama for each and every one of us: it is that we arrive on the earth "trailing clouds of glory" and then, unaccountably, our glory is rejected.

The glory of a child is his innocent purity, within which he carries a truly wondrous set of appetites, spontaneities, angers, desires, and drives. This is his gift to his parents. Sadly, his parents may find they don't want that gift, at least not in the form it arrived.

Maybe what they really wanted was a "nice" boy or girl who would do more or less what they desired, who would follow in their image, perhaps. A child who would be convenient for them, and fit in with their lifestyle. A child who was what they had hoped for, not the one they actually got. And so they unconsciously set about making their child into something else.

That's not unusual. To a greater or lesser degree each of us was diverted from our own path, the one which would have led us to express our true nature: our birthright.

Now, as adults, we may feel an urge to find our real selves by seeking out this true path and seeing where it takes us. That's a choice summed up for me in Robert Frost's poem, *The Road Not Taken*, where he writes:

"Two roads diverged in a wood, and I –
I took the one less travelled by
And that has made all the difference."

It's not that our parents were malevolent – it's just that they needed us to fulfil a particular role in their lives. As Robert Bly so painfully observed, "Our parents rejected us before we could talk, so the pain of the rejection is probably stored in a preverbal place." This is why "Healing The Shadow", "Emotional Process Work", and "Shadow Work" are so powerful – these are techniques which get right to the heart of the issue, quickly, safely and powerfully.

You may be thinking that the concept of a shadow bag sounds like a "one size fits all" kind of idea. But while the principle is the same for all of us – we have a shadow bag and we put into it the parts of ourselves that are not acceptable – the details differ from person to person.

For example, if you put aspects of your sexuality into the bag when you were a child you've likely suppressed a lot of your natural energy as well. Equally, a man who put his inner feminine, his Anima, into his shadow bag during childhood might not show much of his compassion, emotional vulnerability and softness. A woman who put her masculinity, her Animus, into the bag as a kid may have lost a lot of her energy and drive in the world.

Did you ever stop to wonder how many of your strengths and weaknesses are the result of the unconscious decisions you made to please others?

One client told me over and over that he had no artistic talent whatsoever, even though his dad was a successful artist. Eventually we discovered he'd made a choice early on in life not to "compete" with his dad, for his dad was a jealous and petty man who hated "artistic rivals", as he put it.

Another client who came "to rediscover fun in his life" and who described himself as "a real klutz at sport" told me he gave up his passion for soccer at the age of fourteen because his father was a professor who praised him only for his academic achievements. His dad, he told me, with all the pain of a little boy craving his father's love and approval, had never expressed any interest at all in his sporting prowess: "He never came to a single match. Never once congratulated me on scoring a goal." Many other men have told me that their fathers never once said "I love you, son."

Such are the twists of fate which determine whether we choose to take the road less travelled – or not.

Is your road through life your own choice or someone else's? And how would you know, anyway? Think back, and it may become clear. Some of my clients tell me they can remember a specific moment when they decided something important about themselves which shaped their future.

One man came for therapy because of his lack of trust. He was able to describe a moment in school when the "teacher" hurled the old-fashioned chalk board eraser made of wood at him, hitting him on the head. The class laughed long and hard, no doubt relieved they were not the victims that day. In that moment, he said, he could actually remember making a decision never to trust anyone in authority again.

Another client was twelve when he took home his wounded heart after being beaten with a gym shoe at school for copying his friend's homework – this being in the 1970s, when it was acceptable in England for teachers to hit children in their "care". When he told his parents of his emotional and physical pain, describing how a teacher had thrashed him with a gym shoe on the buttocks, they replied: "If a teacher hit you, you must have done something to deserve it." He told me that he remembered, in that moment, deciding he would never again trust his parents nor confide anything of importance in them.

What Did You Repress Into Your Shadow?

A child can repress many aspects of his or her personality in one or more of the four archetypal quarters.

In the Warrior quarter, that might include anger, fierceness, determination, boundary setting, and being fully present in the world. Someone who put this kind of energy into shadow as a child might look like a victim, someone who can be pushed around, a walkover, in adult life.

However, the energy of those qualities doesn't go away, even after years in shadow. In fact, with the right stimulation, in the right circumstances, the energy of these repressed Warrior qualities can explode as violence and rage. Equally, it can be unconsciously turned against the self, producing feelings of depression, passivity and hopelessness.

In the Lover quarter, a boy might put his compassion, love, sensitivity, desire for connection, and tenderness into the shadow bag. Again the energy doesn't go away; later in life it may express itself as an addiction, or as narcissism, neediness, an endless sequence of failed relationships, a lack of true connection, or stoicism.

In the quarter of the Magician, qualities such as reasoning ability, intelligence, comprehension, understanding, and intellect may go into shadow. Maybe a child finds it's wiser, or safer, to hide his cleverness, and so he decides to adopt a strategy of appearing dull, even stupid, in his childhood world. Later in life, the energy of those qualities may come back out of shadow as some kind of limiting fear, sometimes as a cynical attitude of superiority and knowingness, sometimes as a blank, overarching sense of confusion in which there are no answers and nothing is clear, and sometimes as endless cyclical thinking which never reaches any useful conclusion.

More than anything else you, like almost everyone else, will have put most, maybe all, of your magnificence, potency, and power, the energy of your Sovereign, into shadow. These are your own natural clouds of glory, the ones which came with you on the day you arrived on the planet. This energy, locked in your shadow bag for much of your life, can become twisted into grandiosity, emerging as an inflated opinion of yourself, a sense of superiority and an air of arrogance, or a sense of inferiority.

Robert Bly wrote *A Little Book On The Human Shadow* back in 1988. He pointed out that there are collective shadow bags available for those who care to pick them up and help to fill them: a bag for each town, community, family, religion, social group – they all have their own shadow bags. As Bly said, it's almost as if certain groups of people make an unconscious, collective, psychic decision to put certain types of energy into their own shadow bag.

In this book he also suggested that an American citizen who was curious to know what might be in the national shadow bag at that time could find out by listening to what a State Department official said when he criticized Russia. Nowadays Russia may not be the object of our unconscious fears, but there are plenty of other unwilling countries which serve as the targets of our repressed shadow energies. How little has changed over time! The shadow energies do indeed go full circle, finding similar targets from one generation to the next.

And while some of us might bemoan the pressure to be a certain way, and see it as a by-product of modern civilization, Robert Bly shrewdly observed that even the most traditional cultures have always had a different but perhaps even larger shadow bag all of their own.

In fact many non-westernized cultures have always put individuality, creativity and inventiveness into their shadow bags. This cultural pressure was required because conformity and tribal loyalty, rather than freedom of individual expression, was needed to ensure survival.

A final point about your own shadow bag: you can only see its contents by careful observation. Some useful questions to help discover what's in your bag include: what, or who, triggers a strong emotional reaction in you – especially when you feel compelled to justify your reaction? Do you react to certain events in your life with a level of force and energy which is way out of line with the stimulus? In what circumstances do you find you simply can't stop yourself reacting in a certain way, even when you don't want to?

If you don't understand why you react a certain way, here are some practical clues to identifying your own shadows.
• To start with, at some point you may recall making a decision not to behave in a certain way or not to like a particular person.
• Later in life, you find yourself acting that way "by accident".
• And to cap it all, the behaviour seems as if it's controlling you, rather than the other way round.

Often, you feel as if the energy behind the behaviour somehow isn't even a part of you, almost as if it comes from somewhere else. But even though it seems unwanted and unknown, it still feels curiously compelling. Of course it does – this is energy which came from within you and was somehow disowned by you. Now it wants – and needs – to be owned by you once again so it can assume its original form and purpose.

Projection: A Way To Explore Your Shadow

Projection is a way in which we can ignore the existence of certain qualities in ourselves while attributing them to others. It's one of the ways we defend ourselves against awareness of the energies we've put into shadow, both positive and negative. For example, a man who has put his anger into shadow – in other words who is unconsciously angry – may constantly accuse other people of being angry. It's easier for him to see anger as living in others than it is to admit it lives in him.

His emotional growth is all about coming to terms with the reality that anger lives inside him, albeit in shadow, and reintegrating its energy into his personality in a conscious, healthy way. This is the essence of personal growth and development; it is a necessary step to regain control over the way you express your emotions.

The more deeply repressed a shadow energy is within your unconscious, the harder it will be for you to identify and own your projections. So those accusations of racism, sexism, immaturity, infidelity, untrustworthiness, disloyalty and lack of love which you fling at your spouse, your colleagues, your neighbours and your kids – well, better be careful, for those qualities might just be alive and well and living inside you.

And those awful behaviours and emotions you see so often in others? Forget for a moment what you see in others; the real question is this: what are you missing in yourself as you point out other people's failings?

Get the idea? We all do this; and we do it all the time. And we never know we're doing it until we start to examine our shadows.

Sigmund Freud was probably the first therapist, historically, to explain this phenomenon. He had it right when he said that the thoughts, motivations, desires, and feelings which we cannot accept as our own, as belonging to us, can be mentally placed in the world outside of us and attributed to someone else.

This is a great way of avoiding ownership of your thoughts, feelings and actions. Such ownership could remind you of the need to take responsibility for the consequences of your actions. And this might encourage you to do some personal work on yourself. Sure, it's *easier* not to do the work, but the world around you will pay a price for your indifference as the energy in your shadow bag continues to leak out and splatter messily over your friends and family.

And let's face it, you'll pay a price too: not just all those moments of hurt, of shame, of difficulty with your loved ones, of failed expectations, of fear limiting you, of low self-esteem, but also the mysterious re-appearance of exactly what you don't want in your life, over and over again.

But here's an interesting thing. Projection isn't arbitrary. It seizes on something you see in another person, and the seed of truth in what you see becomes the basis on which you can generously "give them" all of your disowned material.

There's something else important about projection too – it can lead to idealization.

When you project your Sovereign energy outwards onto another (in other words, you see your own gold in someone else, rightly or wrongly), you are idealizing them. Idealization is a necessary step in childhood emotional development – children tend to idealize their parents – and it is part of the early stages of falling in love. You might think, though, that it's better, on balance, to keep your glory for yourself, particularly if you want to be an emotionally healthy adult with power and presence in the world.

Carl Jung explained how the parts of our personality we hold in shadow are likely to give rise to projection. As he said, projection can happen on a small-scale, one to one basis, or on a national or international basis. So when unstable, immature and unpredictable national "leaders" start projecting their shadows onto each other the rest of us had better watch out.

Another form of projection in our society has become known as "victim blaming". This is particularly common with the victims of sexual assault. This is where the victim is criticized or blamed for having somehow been responsible for the perpetrator's actions.

We victim blame because it makes us feel safer.

Any story of misfortune, particularly those involving violence or harm, can impact us at a deep level. Human beings are empathic creatures, and when we hear a story about another person we tend to consciously or unconsciously project ourselves into the story to understand how we'd feel and what we could potentially learn from the story. We can also project our own fear into the story.

That happens when we imagine how it might feel to be the victim – we then feel some fear, or at least some lack of safety. After all, if it happened to them, it could surely happen to us.

So to recreate a sense of safety we project the victim within us, the part of us which fears attack, onto the other person. They then become culpable and we are relieved of our fears.

Maybe that's why so many TV programs feature horrific stories of murder, death and suffering. Why else would we watch such things? Where is the reward, the motivation for watching, if it is not to project our fear outwards and so relieve our emotional burden?

Yes indeed; but there is another dimension to this. Inside each of us there is a potential perpetrator, a part of us capable of inflicting harm and damage on others. To the extent that we were victimized by others, whether that took the form of emotional, physical, or sexual harm, so we may carry the energy of the perpetrator.

Such hostile energy is often repressed and denied because it is both socially unacceptable and difficult for us even to admit to ourselves that we carry it. But when we carry that energy in shadow it will leak out, perhaps as a defence of the perpetrator's actions, perhaps as victim blaming, and perhaps as active persecution of another person in some way. This happens because the energy of the perpetrator is within us.

When we hear about violence, victimization and similar events on TV or see them in the movies, or when we read about them on our internet home page every day, perhaps we're unconsciously seeking out a mirror for the part of ourselves which we prefer not to know about and keep under wraps by telling ourselves: "I couldn't possibly do that."

One client told me how he was "overtaken by a fit of madness" when he found himself "unable" to stop accusing his wife of being unfaithful. The irony was startling, for in fact he was the one who was actually having an affair. This is a classic projection, attributing blame to an innocent person; for how much easier it is to project the guilt and shame of your own infidelity onto your wife than to admit what lies within yourself.

Likewise, a bully may unconsciously project his own vulnerability onto the target of his bullying behaviour. He can then act out aggressively against the victim while not feeling his own insecurity and vulnerability. Such aggressive projections can occur anywhere from the micro-level of interpersonal relationships all the way up to the macro-level of international politics and armed conflict between nations.

A final example of negative projection is the way in which people can project their own internal harsh judgements or conscience onto another person. This kind of projection can lead to false accusations of personal or political misconduct.

We project our positive qualities onto others as well. Many of us do not allow ourselves to see our positive energies such as optimism, hope, intelligence, power, presence, potency, and creativity. Instead we disown them and project them onto others.

Projection keeps you safe in some way by not allowing you to see the things about yourself which are – or were once – too frightening or painful (or magnificent) to fully own. However, when you project what is really your energy onto others, the less energy you have available for yourself. When you take back the projections you've placed on others, you stop seeing them through the filter of your own shadow. You see them as they really are.

Not only that, but when you take back your projections you grow more in your own emotional maturity, simply because you are making yourself more complete, more whole.

You may have come to believe that you simply do not possess the energies repressed into your shadow bag. You don't even think twice about what's going on when you spot these qualities in others and don't feel them in yourself. But the truth is, you are projecting your energy, repressed or not, and you're diminishing your power by giving it away.

Conversely, you serve yourself by reintegrating shadow energy into your conscious awareness. You can make it part of the person you are today – and if necessary, you can also transform the energy of shadow back into a more positive form and reclaim once more the gold it originally contained.

There are some areas where this process of reintegration is particularly important: sexuality is high on that list. If you don't feel much interest in sex, while surrounded by others whose sexuality seems to be obvious and keenly expressed, you might be disowning your own sexual energy and seeing it in someone else. Equally, if you feel disgusted about other people's sexual antics, maybe the disgust you're really avoiding is disgust at your own sexual drives and urges?

Discovering what projections you've put on others is always interesting. Sometimes it can be quite challenging, but it's always rewarding.

Another benefit of owning your projections is the energy you'll gain. This is the energy of repression and denial which you no longer need to use in keeping your shadow energies locked away within you. This is energy which becomes available for you to consciously use in running your life.

Years ago, I took part in a series of ten-day-long, residential integrative therapy workshops during which each participant had the opportunity to do one or two pieces of deep emotional healing work alongside the theory and teaching. As soon as I set foot in the room on the first day, I could sense something tangibly different about the energy of my fellow participants. They all seemed to have a much greater presence than most people I knew at the time.

When I discovered how much personal therapy these men and women had undertaken, I knew I'd found the answer: they'd been in therapy for ten, fifteen, even twenty years. It's so obvious, now, as I look back. Yet this was the first time I'd experienced the way in which reclaiming the energy of repression and projection can produce a far more powerful way of being present in the world.

The best way to reclaim this energy for yourself is to attend a workshop where you can discover what you've hidden, repressed and denied, and then start the work of reclaiming the cut-off energies in your shadow bag.

You'll find this will rapidly eliminate your more dysfunctional and unhelpful behaviours and help you get much more control over your thoughts, feelings, and actions. You'll also develop a lot more control and choice over how you react to others, even when you're under extreme provocation.

Transference

Transference is something that develops between two people when one of them unconsciously "sees" the other as a significant person from their past. Transference can develop during therapy or counselling when the therapist seems to assume the identity of some historical figure in the client's life. That's common enough, but transference is much wider than this.

When anyone in your life reminds you in some way of a historical figure in your life with whom you still have "unresolved issues" or emotional "baggage", then you may start reacting to them as if they really are that person from your past.

Perhaps your boss at work reminds you of your difficult and challenging father or your brother, and you find yourself responding to your boss just like you did to your dad or brother all those years ago. Now there's a dynamic that will most likely create difficulties for you!

Or maybe your girlfriend or wife reminds you of your mother, at least in certain ways, and you gradually become aware that you're responding to her as if she is indeed your mother. This, as you may already know, is generally not helpful in an intimate relationship!

Then again, you might find you have a work colleague or a friend who seems to irritate you, just as your annoying younger sibling tried your patience to the limits all those years ago in your family.

While this kind of transference can be useful in revealing where you have unresolved emotional issues to work on, there's also a problem: you're not really connecting with the person currently in your life. Rather, you're relating to them through a filter – through the memory of someone else which has been triggered for some reason or other.

The key here is to go beyond the transference, to find a way to step out of it somehow, so you can see the people in your life today as they really are, not as some reflection of your past.

The unconscious is very powerful. It seeks out people who embody the energy of those with whom we have unresolved issues from earlier in our lives. This is what Freud called the repetition compulsion: an unconscious drive to achieve resolution of the outstanding emotional issues you have with a historical figure in your life, by finding someone who resembles them in your current life.

(What this means is that when you have outstanding issues with your mother, you might find yourself repeatedly encountering and getting involved with women who behave like your mother!)

One way to stop this happening, to prevent the emotional regression that makes you feel like a little boy again and which makes your power in the world melt away, is to find a woman with whom you really can work out these difficulties. Of course that's not always so easy without professional help, because you're right in the middle of the emotional drama when it breaks out, and you may well regress to your childhood ways of being in the world.

A more useful and potentially transformative alternative is to take part in an Emotional Process Workshop where you can do some work on your shadow (see page 179). With the help of the facilitators and the other group members, you can set up a representation of your childhood experience and replay events from the past in symbolic form. This time, though, the object of the work is for you to experience a more positive and empowering outcome.

What happens in such a workshop? Simply, where you were once wounded, now you will be blessed. Where you were once unheard or unappreciated, now you will be honoured. Where you were rejected, you will find acceptance. The feelings you suppressed will be brought out, given space and time to express themselves, and restored to you. By transforming the energy held in your shadow in this way, you will be better able to express yourself in the way that you wish, as the mature man you now are, when similar situations arise in your life today. This is the true nature of Shadow Work.

Each time you do this work, you will reclaim more of the energy you put into shadow, you will feel more powerful, and you will get more control over your life.

This can seem like magic, but there's a beautifully simple and elegant explanation of why this works so well: the techniques used in this work will effectively "reprogram" your brain with a positive and empowering outcome for you. This also gives you a new set of beliefs about yourself. You come to know you are a potent and powerful man, and you embody that belief in all you do.

To put it another way, you go away from the workshop with a set of beliefs about yourself which expand rather than limit your way of being in the world.

This is what is meant by the words "healing your shadow" or "Shadow Work": taking out of your unconscious mind the thoughts, feelings and behaviours caused by traumatic, painful or damaging emotional wounds during your childhood, and putting in place a different emotional "program" which allows you to step around or beyond the limitations of the past and assume your rightful power, presence and potency in the world. We'll look more at this process in the next chapter.

Chapter 7

Emotional Process Work: Becoming Who You Were Always Meant To Be

Imagine that when you were a child your mother was too concerned with her own emotional wounds and difficulties to provide you with the loving care and attention you deserved. Maybe she was openly hostile or conveyed the message she didn't love you. Ever since then you've found it hard to trust women or to open yourself fully in an intimate relationship.

Intuitively you know this lack of trust and openness arises because somewhere inside you there's a young and tender "inner child", a part of you which was wounded by your mother's actions. You also intuitively realize that as an adult man, making yourself vulnerable to women may lead to you re-experiencing that pain.

Or maybe you don't realize that, because every time you get into a relationship, the same thing happens – you get hurt again, or you regress and begin to feel like a little boy frustrated with his mummy. That's because of some unconscious beliefs about women which developed during childhood and which still lie inside you, om shadow, waiting for the right trigger before they make you regress into little boy mode. No matter how powerful you really are, there are circumstances which can stop you standing in your mature masculinity. In fact, you feel powerless in the presence of a woman who behaves like your mummy did, all those years ago.

But why? At some time, for some very good reason, you unconsciously created a set of beliefs about how you "have" to be when you're in a relationship with a woman if you're to get love, or what passes for love. And this was most likely shaped by what you learned about relationships with women from being with your mother or other important and significant women in your life.

No matter what the particular circumstances you faced in your own life, this example illustrates how we all behave in ways which recreate emotional challenges or emotional pain, without really understanding why. Fact is, there are as many personal issues which men and women may want to work on as there are men and women in the world. Speaking of which, what are we actually dealing with here? What can you explore, resolve, heal, rebalance or repair when you do this kind of Shadow Work? Here are a few ideas:

Abandonment, loss of loved ones, lack of love. Shame, humiliation, disrespect. Boarding school. Bullying. Issues with sexuality. Lack of sexual interest. Absent fathers (oh, the number of men who had inadequate or absent fathers). Absent mothers. Smothering mothers. Narcissistic mothers. Angry mothers. Abuse, be it sexual, physical, or emotional. Your lack of leadership in your own life. Not knowing what you want, or not knowing how to get what you want. A sense of powerlessness, impotence or inadequacy. Lack of self esteem. Poor boundaries, an inability to say "No" (or "Yes"). Lack of assertiveness. Not knowing what love is or how to find it. Being overwhelmed by the need for love. Inability to stand up to the masculine. Inability to stand firm in the face of the feminine. Not feeling masculine, or feeling too feminine. Not feeling anything. Dysfunctional behaviour. Loneliness. Lack of friendships. Rage, grief, despair. Anxiety and fear. Not seeing any reason to live. Finding a purpose in life. Compulsions and addictions. Unmourned losses and the grief you carry.

Well, you get the idea: just about anything.

Emotional process workshops are one setting in which you can "work" on your shadow, or if you prefer, "heal" your shadow. In such a workshop, participants and facilitators start by getting to know and trust each other, so the group develops both strength and safety; enough safety for men and women to explore their problems and challenges, and their desire for change, without the fear of being hurt once again.

Most importantly, we create a safe "container" in which men (and women in our mixed groups) are respected and in control of what happens at all times. This is the container in which you can work on your shadow. This is the container in which you are "held" as you explore the parts of yourself which carry your emotional wounds.

There are many techniques which allow us, together, to replay the drama of your past, but this time to give it a different outcome. It's like rewriting the last act of the play so that you get the outcome you desire. In the example at the start of this chapter, this might be the ability to open up to women and show your vulnerability so that you can give and receive love fully, openly and without feeling fear.

The results of Emotional Process Workshops can be almost miraculous because the Shadow Work goes right back to the heart of your deepest emotional issues. And these techniques work *fast* because they are action-oriented and direct. In fact, I believe that a 90 minute session of deep personal work in a group setting, a safe space where you can re-enact parts of your life's drama and experience a different outcome, can be as effective as several sessions of weekly one-to-one counselling or therapy.

One To One Work On Your Shadow

A very good alternative to group work is to do your emotional healing work in a one-to-one setting with an experienced facilitator, a shadow healer who is well versed in working with these emotional wounds and issues.

Sure, the techniques are different, but the outcome is just as dramatic: you can quickly resolve the issues and challenges that are affecting the quality of your life.

How do group work and individual work compare? The most obvious benefit of working in a group is that you are not alone; you are witnessed and supported. Most of the wounds which men and women experienced during childhood were borne alone, so to be witnessed in your personal healing work in a group can be a powerful restorative and reparative experience in itself. In addition, each group can generate a very special heart-centred energy which helps to hold the participants in a sense of emotional security and hasten their emotional transformation.

The obvious benefit of working one to one is that you can move at the pace which suits you best. The session is more focused on you, and you have the full attention of the facilitator for as long as you are in the room.

Perhaps the best way of doing your work is to combine a series of personal sessions with a group session every three months or so. This seems to really speed up progress for most people.

To recap:

There are some clear signs if you are dealing with shadow energies in your life:

First, once upon a day you made a choice not to be a certain way in the world. You did this for a very good reason, usually concerned with maintaining your "safety" in your family or some other highly charged setting like boarding school. That safety may have been emotional, physical or spiritual.

Second, consciously or unconsciously, you put certain unwanted thoughts, feelings and behaviours into your shadow bag.

Third, you find this energy sometimes bursts out in your life today, uncontrollably and unexpectedly. Often it looks different to when it went into your shadow bag.

Fourth, when it does burst out, it feels as if the energy is in control of you. It may even feel as if it has no connection with you. ("Where did that come from?")

Which all adds up to this: when an energy goes into shadow, it grows, and later in life when you find yourself in a situation – as you surely will – which mirrors the original situation in your childhood in some way, you'll find yourself behaving in a way you don't want to behave, doing what you don't want to do, and saying things you don't want to say. All apparently without any control.

You might find yourself shouting at your children, your wife or your girlfriend, thinking awful thoughts about hitting your children, cowering in front of a dominant boss, allowing people to walk all over you, not speaking up when you need to, experiencing violent images and thoughts, crying uncontrollably – and a million and one other unhelpful things.

In either a group workshop or a one-to-one setting you can dive deep into the causes of these behaviours and explore and understand them. Then you can literally embody a different way of being in the world: a more authentic, genuine and balanced way of being. A way of being which reflects who you really are.

Men who work on their shadow in this way discover that when they're in a provocative or triggering situation they have more control over how they respond. This lets them consciously choose how to respond to situations and events which would previously have "triggered" them to react without thinking.

That's the difference – in the past you would have just reacted without much control as shadowy energy burst or maybe even exploded out of you, most likely leaving you feeling bad afterwards. When you've worked on your shadow you'll find you can choose how to respond to events. You'll develop mastery of your old behaviour patterns and be able to change them into something much more helpful for your life today. What's most amazing is that almost any historical experience can be transformed in this way.

There are facilitation techniques which allow you to work on an emotional issue without having to explain the historical details, if that's better for you. Such techniques can help with all kinds of abuse where you may not wish to reveal the details of what happened to you.

These workshops are also an effective way to develop the power of an archetype if you don't have enough strength in that area.

Suppose you want to strengthen your Warrior so you can set boundaries with people – which might mean finding ways to say a clear "No" or a definite "Yes". You can start by finding out how and why (and by whom) the power to set boundaries was taken away from you; then you can develop the ability to set clear boundaries effectively.

Or suppose your issue is not feeling good enough. You might start exploring this, and discover that you came to believe you were not good enough because your father never praised you or was never satisfied with your achievements.

So you might set up a dynamic where you receive blessing and approval from the ideal loving father you never had. This is a profound process, for the part of you still looking out for a Dad's love and approval will accept it eagerly. What happens then? Your sense of self-worth and self-esteem will immediately rise and your beliefs about yourself will change, so that suddenly you know, with a certainty you've never experienced before, that you are indeed worthy of praise, attention, and love.

Just one more example: if you're having difficulties in your relationship with a loved one, you could go a long way to resolving those difficulties with a piece of work in which you explore the origins of your current beliefs, feelings and behaviours. As you explore how these things started, you bring the energy which drove them to come into existence out of shadow and into your awareness.

Then you can own it fully. As you do this, you will gain new power and control which allows you to respond in a different and much more adult way to what happens in your relationship today.

As I suggested before, in Emotional Process Work, when you're working on healing your shadow, you embrace what has been repressed and denied. You embrace it, you bring it into your conscious awareness, and you discover how to control it as servant rather than master. And it works! In over twenty years of working in the world of therapy, I have never seen a more powerful and effective system of personal growth and development than working on your shadow in this way.

But there's more to these workshops than resolving emotional issues from your past, important though that is. You can also enhance and develop the energies which are a bit lacking in you. For example, if you're out of touch with any of your emotions, you can find ways of accessing those emotions and experiencing them fully.

If you aren't sure how to set boundaries with somebody, or you don't know how to express your needs, wishes and desires, you can discover ways to do this in the safe workshop space or in one to one work with a skilled facilitator.

If you can't understand why your life seems limited in some ways, or you can't find ways to get what you want, you can explore the energy that's holding you back. Often the limiting factor is a strategy designed by your Magician archetype and intended to keep you safe during childhood. Sure, that may have served you well in the past, but today – well, it's not necessarily so useful!

Ways of being in the world which you learned when you were five, seven, or ten years old need to be updated so you can transform them into something much more useful in your life today. Together, you and your facilitator can find ways to encourage the part of you that's dedicated to keeping you safe (but is stuck in the past) to turn his attention to doing something much more relevant and helpful for you in your life as an adult man.

As you see, Emotional Process Work is versatile and offers almost unlimited possibilities for change, but through it all runs a single theme: *it will help you become the person you were always meant to be, before the world got in the way*. If you're interested in Emotional Process Work or Shadow Work workshops, which are focused on the art of "Healing Your Shadow", please check out the next chapter of the book.

Chapter 8

Resources: Places To Work On Your Shadow

Here's a selection of facilitators who are well trained and experienced in working with the shadow and emotional issues from the past and present. Each of them has provided some information about how they approach their work.

Groups For Men (UK)

Rod Boothroyd, Diarmaid Fitzpatrick & Ed Rooke run regular Shadow Workshops for men.

They also offer one to one coaching, and you can find details about that lower down the page.

The current group workshops they have scheduled for men are listed on **https://www.strongfreemen.co.uk**

Rod: "I work with men individually and in groups to heal the wounds of childhood in every Archetype. And beyond healing, I work with men to guide them as they explore and access their unexpressed power and potency in the world. Together we explore unconscious shadows, find ways to heal them, and strengthen the power and potency of your Sovereign, the leader within you. I've worked with hundreds of men in groups and one to one settings over the past few years, bringing my training in psychotherapy to complement my vast experience and training in working with the shadow."
Website: https://www.strongfreemen.co.uk
Phone: 01373 455 356
Email: rod@strongfreemen.co.uk

Diarmaid: "As a Certified Shadow Work Facilitator, I see my role as being about enabling people to identify and break free of long standing limiting beliefs and behaviours. By doing so they can lead more enjoyable, fulfilling and purposeful lives. Of all the personal development skills I've learned over many years of personal development I find Shadow Work to be the most effective because it reveals the deeper issues underpinning life's challenges, helps heal old wounds and transforms long standing traumas."
Website: https://www.strongfreemen.co.uk

Ed: "I first became interested in the power of emotional healing as it allowed me to recover from a chronic illness 15 years ago. Since this time I have been deeply engaged with many meditative and therapeutic disciplines, as well as formal training in Psychology (PhD), Hypnotherapy, Generative Coaching and Shadow Work. My approach has also been greatly influenced through extensive training with relationship expert Jan Day. I offer a unique sensitivity and presence in the way I work which often allows clients to rediscover the subtle parts of their unconscious which underlie their recurrent patterns. I care deeply about helping men reconnect with lost parts of themselves, so that they can rediscover who they truly are."
Website: https://www.edrooke.com

*****

Groups For Women (UK)

Please contact Marianne Hill to check what she currently has scheduled. Read more about Marianne on the next page.

Website: https://www.healingtheshadow.co.uk
Phone: 01373 300 749
Email: MarianneHillShadowWork@gmail.com

*****

Mixed Gender Group Work (UK)

1) Marianne Hill and Rod Boothroyd offer a wide variety of workshops for mixed gender groups, including closed groups which meet regularly over six or twelve months, as well as intensive residential workshops.

Website: https://www.healingtheshadow.co.uk
Phone: 01373 300 749
Email: MarianneHillShadowWork@gmail.com

Marianne: "I believe deeply in the transformative power of non-judgemental acceptance – where all parts of us are welcomed, heard and compassionately held. Only then can the most vulnerable parts of ourselves come forward into the light, knowing it is a safe place to be, and that they may finally be witnessed and transformed. I have been working deeply with the shadow for the last 12 years. Initially working as a Shadow Work Facilitator and Coach, I have adapted, expanded and enriched this work over time. In my Healing The Shadow practice I draw on my other twin passions of relationship work and body work and have created a strong and safe framework of holding which allows profound change to take place and be integrated. I am deeply committed to providing a compassionate and transformative place for people who wish to explore and heal their shadow side."

Rod: "Working with women and men in a mixed group provides a rich and fulfilling opportunity to heal the historical wounds which have arisen between men and women. Add this to the opportunity for individual healing work which gradually restores full emotional health and repairs the emotional wounding we experience at the hands of our families and others, and I believe this work makes the world a safer place for everyone – women, men and children alike."

* * * * *

2) Diarmaid Fitzpatrick & Elizabeth Klyne offer mixed gender workshops in locations in the UK, as well as individual sessions and one-to-one work with male and female clients.

Diarmaid: "I see my role as a Certified Shadow Work facilitator as being about enabling people to identify and break free of long standing limiting beliefs and behaviours. By doing so they can lead more enjoyable, fulfilling and purposeful lives. Of all the personal development skills I've learned over many years of personal development I find Shadow Work to be the most effective because it reveals the deeper issues underpinning life's challenges, helps heal old wounds and transforms long standing traumas."
Email: d.fitzpatrick@awarenessbd.com
Phone: 07768 468 031

Elizabeth: "I've been delighted to create a safe and shame-free environment in which people can find empathy, take possession of their gifts and talents and access the power that flows from coming to terms with the truth of any situation. I find myself consistently in awe of our ability to survive, heal and flourish in the face of the challenging circumstances and beliefs that we all encounter, and blessed to be present in those moments of transformation."
Email: eklyne@me.com
Phone: 07801 374 589

* * * * *

You can find other facilitators by searching for
shadow work workshops
and
shadow work consultations
online.

* * * * *

Resources: Places To Work On Your Shadow

One-to-One Work (UK)

Rod Boothroyd offers one-to-one work with both men and women. You can see more information about Rod on page 179.
Websites:
https://www.takeyourpower.co.uk
https://www.thebalancedwhole.com
Phone: 07788 502 902
Email: rod@takeyourpower.co.uk

Diarmaid Fitzpatrick offers one-to-one sessions with both women and men. You can see more information about Diarmaid on pg. 180.
Email: d.fitzpatrick@awarenessbd.com
Mobile: 07768 468 031

Marianne Hill offers one-to-one work with both women and men. You can see more information about Marianne on page 181.
Website: https://healingtheshadow.co.uk
Phone: 01373 300 749
Email: MarianneHillShadowWork@gmail.com

Elizabeth Klyne offers one-to-one work with both women and men. You can see more information about Elizabeth on page 182.
Email: eklyne@me.com
Phone: 07801 374 589

Ed Rooke offers one-to-one sessions with both women and men. You can see Ed's details on page 180.
Website: https://www.edrooke.com
Phone: 07753 172 419

* * * * *

USA & Other Locations

You can find a list of facilitators who work in the USA and other countries by searching on Google.com for "Shadow Work USA", "Shadow Work Germany", and so on.

* * * * *

Organizations You May Find Helpful

The ManKind Project (www.mkp.org) offers a wide variety of men's experiences all designed to help men grow. Here's an extract from their website: "A men's community for the 21st Century, the ManKind Project has three decades of proven success hosting life-changing experiential personal development programs for men... and supports a global network of free men's groups. MKP also supports men in leading lives of integrity, authenticity, and service. We believe that emotionally mature, powerful, compassionate, and purpose-driven men will help heal some of our society's deepest wounds. We support the powerful brilliance of men. We are willing to look at, and take full responsibility for, the pain we are also capable of creating - and suffering. We care deeply about men, our families, communities, and the planet." MKP hosts its transformative events in many countries worldwide, including the UK, several European countries, and Israel.

Celebration of Being (www.celebrationofbeing.co.uk) is an organization devoted to healing the emotional wounds of men and women, and is at the forefront of inner growth work. They say: "We are committed to providing an unforgettable journey into the depth and beauty of your true self – your being – especially through the doorway of male-female relationships. Our one-of-a-kind Rites of Passage workshops are designed to heal the wounds that are keeping you separate from yourself, from the opposite gender and from God. Our intention is not to conquer the shadow part of ourselves, but to draw it out into the light of our awareness and compassion. Our workshops illuminate the glory of man and woman. To date more than two thousand participants from all over the world have made this incredible journey with us from all age groups, all faiths, all races and all walks of life."

Videos You May Find Helpful

You can see a series of videos on Shadow Work & the various archetypes on YouTube. You can access the first video in the series as well as a complete play list for all these videos quickly and easily with this shortcut URL:
https://tinyurl.com/healingtheshadow

Books You May Find Helpful

How to Be An Adult: A Handbook on Psychological And Spritual Integration by David Richo

This is a super little book whose title could easily be "How to Be The Sovereign In Your Own Life". He explains the characteristics of emotional maturity and suggests easy and simple ways to grow those qualities in your life.

Owning Your Own Shadow by Robert A Johnson

An exploration of the dark or hidden aspect of the persona - what it is, how it originates, how it is formed, and how it can be used to bring wholeness to the personality.

A Little Book on the Human Shadow by Robert Bly

Robert Bly explains how we are born with "360-degree radiance" and how our spirits shine in all directions. Over the first 20 years or so of our lives we learn to stuff the "bad" parts into a shadow bag so that we become well behaved, more polite, and better able to manage our anger. Sadly for us, we also stuff other things in there too, like our "feminine" or "masculine" sides, or our vitality and energy. Then, to explain why these parts are missing, we learn to say things like "I'm not really a creative-type person." Eventually we begin to miss these parts of ourselves and feel tired from dragging our shadow bags behind us, all the while emotionally struggling to deal with the challenges we face. At this point we have a choice: either to reintegrate our shadows within our psyche or to devote increasing amounts of energy to maintaining our rigidity and repression, all the while becoming more controlling towards, and intolerant of, others.

Iron John by Robert Bly

Robert Bly suggests how the images of adult manhood given by popular culture are worn out, and suggests men can no longer depend on them. *Iron John* searches for a new vision of what a man is or could be, drawing on psychology, anthropology, mythology, folklore and legend. In particular, Bly looks at the importance of the Wild Man, the essence of male energy.

The Drama Of Being A Child: The Search For The True Self by Alice Miller

Alice Miller examines the consequences of repression at personal and social levels, the causes of the physical and psychological harm done to children and how this can be prevented, and the new methods at our disposal for dealing with the consequences of infant traumas.

The Body Never Lies: The Lingering Effects Of Cruel Parenting by Alice Miller

An examination of childhood trauma and its pervasive, debilitating effects. Miller explores the long-range effects of childhood abuse on the body and shows how a child's humiliation, impotence, and bottled rage will manifest as adult illness. This book may help you confront the overt and covert traumas of your childhood.

Shadow Of The Stone Heart: Search For Manhood by Richard Olivier

The day that Richard Olivier's father, actor Laurence Olivier, died marked a crisis point in Richard Olivier's life. Unable to grieve, his involvement with the Men's Movement helped him adjust from isolation to a fuller expression of his grief. This was the beginning of a process of self-exploration that changed his life. This book is both a memoir of Olivier's challenging relationship with his father and an accessible account of the Men's Movement.

Coming Home: Reclaiming and Championing Your Inner Child by John Bradshaw

John Bradshaw explains his tried and tested techniques to reveal the inner child. He explains how the emotional wounds we receive during childhood and adolescence continue to contaminate our adult lives. His techniques, which are explained clearly in this book, help people to reach back to the child inside and heal those wounds. "Three things are striking about inner child work," says John Bradshaw. "The speed with which people change, the depth of that change, and the power and creativity that can result when the wounds from the past are healed."

Fire in the Belly: On Being a Man by Sam Keen

This book is for men who have experienced their emptiness, loneliness, and longing for connection, but whose ways of dealing with these issues are limited by old ways of being and out-of-date beliefs about themselves. This book might well change those beliefs as it introduces us to new ways of seeing masculinity, the world, and men.

Absent Fathers, Lost Sons: The Search for Masculine Identity by Guy Corneau

Many modern men do not seem to be deeply rooted in a sense of their own masculinity. Psychoanalyst Guy Corneau traces this experience to an even deeper feeling men have of their fathers' silence or absence – sometimes a physical absence, but also very often an emotional and spiritual absence. He suggests that our challenges around masculinity stem from the fact that we have lost the masculine initiation rituals that in the past ensured a boy's passage into manhood. In this engaging examination of the many different ways this missing link manifests in men's lives Corneau proposes that for men today, regaining the essential "second birth" into manhood lies in developing the ability to be a father to themselves. This is not only a means of healing psychological pain but also a necessary step in the process of becoming whole.

Radical Wholeness: The Embodied Present and the Ordinary Grace of Being by Philip Shepherd

Radical Wholeness documents the devastation inflicted by lack of mind-body integration on our personal lives and the planet. But the book is also a practical guide for initiating a personal revolution. By finding your way out of your head and reuniting with your body's intelligence you can ground yourself in a wholeness of being that feels and supports the harmonies not just of your life, but of our wakeful world.

The Success Principles 10th Anniversary Edition: How to Get from Where You Are to Where You Want to Be by Jack Canfield (This book can assist you in forming a vision for your future life.)

Jack Canfield, co-creator of the bestselling *"Chicken Soup for the Soul"* series, claims this book can help any man or woman get from where they are now to where they want to be. The techniques in the book show how to form a vision for your life, increase your confidence, tackle daily challenges, live with passion and purpose, and realize all your ambitions. Does it work? Well, apparently this book describes a lot of the ideas and techniques used by the world's most successful men and women. Taken together and practiced every day, these principles can empower you to a new way of being in the world.

Men and the Water of Life: Initiation and the Tempering of Men by Michael Meade (Meade has written many other books of interest to men)

Through myths and ancient stories, Meade takes readers through the stages in a man's life. He focuses on initiation and shows how the stories allow for a new and sometimes radical re-examination of childhood issues from a different perspective. Meade's commitment to men and their healing is obvious, making this a must-read for anyone wishing to gain a deeper understanding of our individual and collective psyches.

About The Author: Rod Boothroyd

I've been involved with personal work and the Men's Movement* in one form or another for over twenty years. Like many other men I found my life collapsing around me at midlife. I realized my life could not continue as I had set it up, and I embarked on a search for what I would now call "soul healing". This took me to Vision Quests in the high mountains of the USA, Richard Rohr's male initiation (Illuman.org), training in Transactional Analysis and Integrative Psychotherapy, an exploration of Shadow Work, backpacking in the wilderness, and other deep personal soul diving work, until, after many other adventures, I found the New Warrior Training Adventure run by the ManKind Poject (mankindproject.org).

Here I discovered a new model of masculinity and – more importantly – a body of men who seemed to relate to life on a different, deeper level. MKP offers a weekend "initiation" into manhood, a Rite Of Passage designed for the 21st century society in which we live. This was a joy! And after my initiation, I joined a group of men from MKP in an ongoing men's group. These men are still among my closest buddies. Over time, I began to explore the human archetypes and how they manifest in men and women, and came to understand the immense power of the archetypal approach to healing emotional wounds. The rest, as they say, is history... some of it not yet written.

*According to Wikipedia:
"The men's movement is a social movement consisting of groups and organizations of men and their allies who focus on gender issues and whose activities range from self-help and support to lobbying and activism. ... The movement exists predominantly in the Western world and emerged in the 1960s and 1970s."

Quotations From The Writings Of Carl Jung

"People will do anything, no matter how absurd, in order to avoid facing their own souls. One does not become enlightened by imagining figures of light, but by making the darkness conscious."
From "Psychology and Alchemy"

"There is no coming to consciousness without pain."
From "Contributions to Analytical Psychology"

"Everything that irritates us about others can lead us to an understanding of ourselves."
From "Memories Dreams and Reflections"

"Knowing your own darkness is the best method for dealing with the darknesses of other people."
From "Letters Volume 1"

"Your vision will become clear only when you can look into your own heart. Without, everything seems discordant; only within does it coalesce into unity. Who looks outside dreams; who looks inside awakes."
From "Letters Volume 1"

"We are living in what the Greeks called the right time for a 'metamorphosis of the gods,' i.e. of the fundamental principles and symbols. This peculiarity of our time, which is certainly not of our conscious choosing, is the expression of the unconscious within us… Coming generations will have to take account of this momentous transformation if humanity is not to destroy itself through the might of its own technology and science."
From "The Undiscovered Self"

Printed in Great Britain
by Amazon